The Shelbourne

and its people

The Shelbourne
and its people

MICHAEL O'SULLIVAN

BERNARDINE O'NEILL

BLACKWATER PRESS

Editor
Joanna McAdam

Design and Layout
Paula Byrne, Liz Murphy

Cover Design
Liz Murphy

ISBN
1 84131 442 0

Produced in Ireland by
Blackwater Press
C/o Folens Publishers
Hibernian Industrial Estate
Tallaght, Dublin 24

To the staff of the Shelbourne, past and present, who make it what it is.

ACKNOWLEDGEMENTS

The authors and the management of the Shelbourne Hotel are grateful for the sponsorship which this project received from Irish Distillers, Limited, Mercury Engineering Limited, Bacchus Wine and Spirit Merchants, and IBM Ireland.

The authors are also grateful for the time, support and practical assistance which was given by Patrick Anderson, Maureen Blair, Mary Brennan, Aodagan Brioscu, The Hon. Garech Browne, Laurence James Browne, Padraic and Terry McCarville Browne, Tom Callary, Peter Cann, Rory Carren, William Cash, Anne Chambers, Michael P. Costelloe, Brian Coyle, Harry Crosby, Melosine Bowes Daly, Richard Davies, Jimmy Dixon, Charles F. Duffy, Mable Enoch, Rosemary Enright, Roy Foster, Earl Gill, Alan Gleeson, the Knight of Glin, Colette Griffin, David Griffin, David Hanly, Adrian Hardiman, Anne Henderson, Henry Henderson, Derrick Hill, Mary Holohan, John Hurt, Jimmy Kelly, Adrian Keogh, Irene Keogh, Harry Latham, Edward J. Law, Derek Mahon, Peter Malone, Paddy Moloney, Peter Molony, Eoin McCann, John Count McCormack, Frank McDonald, Count Randall McDonnell, Gabriel McGovern, Peter McGuire, Orla McLoughlin, P.J. Mara, John Montague, Des Murnane, Patrick Murnane, Michael Murphy, Jacqueline O'Brien, Lawrence P. O'Connor, David O'Ferrall, Frank O'Kane, F.J. O'Reilly, Derek Overend, Sarah Owens, Noel Pearson, Claus Pederson, Sr. Kathleen Power, Robert Poynton, Aidan Prior, Martin S. Quigley, Rev. Fr. Seán Quigley, Patrick Semple, Noel Sheehan, Paddy Shortall, Sam Stephenson, Sophie Tebbit, Gabriel Walsh, Maureen Walsh, Lesley Whiteside.

And to all those members of the Shelbourne staff whose courtesy and assistance contributed so greatly to our comfort while working on this project, Carol Ni Ghabhann's team in the Shelbourne Bar, Derek Byrne, Linda Coughlan, Damien Earley, Aiden Foley, Michael Gall, Ronan Horgan, Michelle Lynch, Jennifer Murphy and David Smith.

Also Pirkko Aavikko, Kristan Burness, Lisa Halton, Jennifer Heenan, Ruth Kane, Ana Laglera, Claire Lawrence, Caroline Mahon, Sharon McGuire, Christine Moutintio, Feargal Ó Dornáin, Sandra Owens and

Jemma Walsh in The Side Door Restaurant, Sean Boyd, Etain Boyd, Charles Brady, James Cully, George Duffy, John Geraghty and Conor McCool in the Horseshoe Bar, Betty O'Neill, Clare Anderson, Audrey Bradley, Maureen Cosgrove, Daphne Cuddy, Xich-Ve Ho, Sarah Jane Madden, Anthony McGuinness, Fiona Murphy, Jackie O'Brien, and Sandra Whelan in the Lord Mayor's Lounge, Declan Saunders, Nicolas Bastouil, Juan Calapell, David Cave, Nicolas Duquairoux, Attilia Gardner, Alexis Hebraud, Bruno Macari, Cristophe Marsan, Dany Nivet, Juan Romero and Maurizio Selvaggio in Number 27 The Green.

Our thanks also to Jim Barry, Liam Batten, Jimmy Corcoran, Trevor Deegan, John Earle, Dominic Fagan, Mary Gallagher, David Johnson, Michael Keogh, Stephen McMahon, Anthony Neary, James O'Keefe, Charles O'Reilly, Garry O'Sullivan, John Reade and Chris Slater at the front desk.

A special word of thanks to accommodation assistant, Riona Skuse, whose tactful ministrations kept the office area civilised for the duration.

Many thanks, also, to Joanna McAdam and Anna O'Donovan at Blackwater Press for their editorial assistance.

In addition, for the use of photographs and other materials, we thank the following: p. 21 Margaret Cotton Jury, younger and older, p. 26 Stephen Cotton Jury, p. 77 Peter Jury (all courtesy of Sophie Tebbit); p. 27, George Moore, Novelist, by John Butler Yeats (National Gallery of Ireland); p. 35 British garrison dismissal parade, p. 43 British troops departing the Shelbourne 1916, p. 46 Captain Andrews and Colonel Madden, p. 48 Cantrell and Cochrane van, p. 49 Barricades outside the Shelbourne, (all courtesy of Paddy Shortall); p. 84 Earl Gill and his band (Earl Gill); p. 85 Shelbourne chefs (Alan Gleeson); p. 91 Gabirel Walsh on his prom night (Gabriel Walsh); p. 111 Princess Grace and Noel Sheehan (Noel Sheehan); p. 116 Derek Mahon, p. 127 John Hurt and the Hon. Garech Browne, p. 179 Jimmy Corcoran outside the Shelbourne, p. 186 Noel Pearson (all courtesy of Sarah Owens); p. 117 Seán Ó Riada (Jeffrey Craig), p. 129, Melosine Bowes Daly (*The Times*), p. 145 Jimmy Dixon coaching his pageboys (*Sunday Mirror*), p. 165 Shelbourne interior after bomb explosion (*The Irish Times*). In other instances, photographs and other materials have come from the Shelbourne archive.

CONTENTS

PREFACE

'Life at the Shelbourne is a thing in itself and a thing to be studied', George Moore observed in his novel *A Drama in Muslin.*

The hotel has made numerous guest appearances in many books but only one full-length study of the Shelbourne has appeared in print. In 1951 Elizabeth Bowen's *The Shelbourne Hotel* was published to critical acclaim in Ireland, Great Britain and in the United States. Miss Bowen's book was a superb evocation of life in the hotel from its foundation in 1824 to World War II. The book was commissioned by Captain Peter Jury. His family association with the Shelbourne began in 1866 when they purchased it from the Burke family who founded it.

The recent discovery of two large collections of important papers relating to the hotel's 175-year history has made this new book possible. One set was found in the basement of the Shelbourne itself and the other amongst the private papers of the late Captain Peter Jury. Together they form not only a near complete picture of the daily workings of one of Europe's leading hotels but also, in many instances, are valuable original sources on Irish history. A collection of letters from the hotel's manager, G.R.F. Olden, to the Shelbourne's owners then resident in England gives a very personal account of the 1916 Rising and the Civil War.

This book is a history of the Shelbourne and some of the many lives which have been touched by it. It is also, in some respects, a history of modern Ireland. The hotel played no small part in the making of modern Irish history. Its founder, Tipperaryman Martin Burke, was a Catholic Nationalist whose lone dissenting voice at the 'staged' trial of Charles Gavan Duffy, saved the Young Ireland leader from a terrible fate. In 1916 the hotel was garrisoned by the British army and in 1922 by the army of the new Free State. Ireland's first Constitution was drafted within its walls. Terrorist bombs disfigured the hotel and risked the lives of its staff and patrons during the Northern troubles. And in recent times important sideline meetings which were of great consequence to the progress of the peace process were held secretly in the hotel.

In few capitals has the life of the city and the country run so closely in tandem with an hotel as has the life of Dublin, Ireland and the Shelbourne. It is a great deal more than 'the most distinguished address in Ireland'. It is an artery through which has passed, and still passes, some of the most interesting lifeblood of the capital.

Through an accident of good fortune nearly all of the hotel's bound registers, up to the introduction of computers, are still extant. So too are the financial records of the hotel. Their discovery, coupled with the discovery of Peter Jury's papers, has enabled the writing of the most comprehensive history to date of 'the grand old lady of Stephen's Green' as she reaches her 175th birthday.

Michael O'Sullivan
The Shelbourne Hotel
October 1999

CHAPTER ONE

MARTIN BURKE'S SHELBOURNE

A fearless patriot, independent Juryman, and a true-hearted Irishman.

Saint Teresa of Avila once compared our life in this world to a night at a second-class hotel. Sadly, we do not know if the motivation of Martin Burke, the founder of the Shelbourne Hotel, lay in his desire to save his customers from the earthly fate described by St Teresa or if his motivation was less lofty. We do know that Mr Burke was an Irish Catholic who came to prominence in Ireland after the repeal, between 1778 and 1792, of the majority of the repressive laws against his co-religionists. Had these laws remained on the statute books, Burke's extraordinary progress in the Dublin business world would otherwise have been hindered, if not made entirely impossible.

He established the Shelbourne in 1824 just five years before the success of Daniel O'Connell's campaign for Catholic Emancipation. There has been a persistently erroneous impression given of the Shelbourne's founder, of his having emerged from a miasma of social indistinction somewhere in County Tipperary. During his lifetime, Burke was undeniably a man of means, of affairs, substance and considerable style. There has been much speculation as to how Burke achieved sufficient financial security to enable him to accumulate a substantial property portfolio in County Dublin, culminating in the acquisition of the leasehold interests in Stephen's Green which became the jewel in his property crown – the Shelbourne Hotel.

Martin Burke was born in Springfield, County Tipperary, in 1788. The exact nature of how he acquired sufficient wealth to establish the hotel in 1824 remains unclear. However, we do know that by 1824, he had sufficient property interests in and around what was then Kingstown (now Dún Laoghaire) to enable him to raise adequate funds to realise his ambition of opening a hotel on the corner of St Stephen's Green and Kildare Street. We also know that he was possessed of sufficient managerial skills to enable him to quickly establish the venture as one of the most prestigious hotels in Ireland.

Two things stood very much in his favour. The first was his friendship with Thomas Gresham, who in 1817 had purchased 21-22 Sackville Street (now O'Connell Street) to open the Gresham Hotel. The second was the rapidly changing social climate in Ireland after the passing of the Act of Union. The new mood in the city, which had so recently lost its parliament, was beginning to affect how the upper echelons of society organised their social life. The economic climate was another matter altogether. With Dublin no longer the 'second city of the Empire', and with power now vested in London, Burke was a brave but insightful man in proposing to venture a vast sum in opening a new hotel.

Gresham's friendship and generosity were important factors in Burke's decision. He had established, north of the river Liffey, just the sort of establishment his friend Burke now wished to found on Stephen's Green, on the south side of the river. In the wake of the indecent haste with which the fleeing aristocracy abandoned their houses on the north side of the river, it soon ceded way to the south side as the most fashionable part of the city.

Martin Burke admired how Thomas Gresham had risen in life. As a baby he was abandoned on the steps of the Royal Exchange in London.

As a youth, he progressed rapidly from the status of household servant to becoming one of Dublin's most successful businessmen. The two friends were providing a similar service in different locations in the city and in surprisingly similar circumstances. They had each acquired individual but adjoining Georgian town houses which they united to afford their guests the sense of luxury and seclusion to be found in a private town residence. This they successfully coupled with the service desired in a first class hotel. Yet Martin Burke was very much aware of the location of his principal opposition in the hotel trade in Dublin.

It came from a neighbouring establishment on Dawson Street, the Royal Hibernian Hotel, which first opened its doors in 1751. Burke had sufficient belief in his own abilities as a financier and arbiter of taste to convince himself – he need convince no other – that he could make a rival establishment on Stephen's Green a success. The site he picked was an imposing corner of the north side of the Green adjoining Kildare Street.

In 1745 friends of the future Duke of Leinster had looked askance when he proposed to have the architect Richard Cassels build him a magnificent town house a few hundred yards away. The concerns of the Duke's friends were understandable. Many of them still perceived Stephen's Green as a place where the spiritual needs of a leper colony were once attended to by the Whitefriars in late medieval times. Others of his lordship's acquaintance may have had more recent memories of being set upon by the large number of brigands who plied their trade in the dark thickets that made up the wide expanse of untamed commonage. All who passed that corner of the Green were aware that the gallows stood nearby. For many years its threatening presence stood at the beginning of Merrion Row. Some passers by no doubt recalled that a brothel keeper named Darkey Kelly was executed there in 1764, others perhaps, that a bishop was executed there for bestiality in 1640. Supporters of the Rebellion of 1798 could hardly forget that the very site of the new hotel was, during its time as a barracks, a notorious place of torture for imprisoned rebels.

Martin Burke's eye however was on the future, not the past. By 1824, when he began acquiring the houses that later made up his Shelbourne Hotel, that part of Dublin was already established as very desirable for both commercial and residential use. The Duke of Leinster's house had, by 1815, become the headquarters of the Royal Dublin Society. The Molesworth family had laid out Kildare Street, and St Stephen's Green had become the object of primarily speculative residential building. Indeed the very site on which the present hotel now stands was the object of such a venture.

The Second Earl of Shelburne.

Upon it originally stood Lord Kerry's house. The building carried that peer's name until, in 1753, he was advanced in the peerage as Earl of Shelburne. The property was left exposed on its west flank when the Molesworth family demolished their house to make way for the opening from the Green to what is present day Kildare Street. Lord Shelburne's house was a large imposing brick building with gardens extending back to stables and out-offices. A Dublin businessman, Luke White, leased the old mansion to the military for use as a barracks in 1798, having purchased the house for £6,000 in 1793. It housed the additional soldiery sent to quell the Rebellion of 1798. Its use as a barracks, until the end of the Napoleonic wars, took a serious toll on the fabric of the building. Quite soon thereafter, it fell into serious disrepair when a great part of it was damaged by fire. For some years, it stood as an irksome eyesore on the Green. Eventually it was pulled down. On the site, Mr White, with a keen eye to its speculative value, built three new houses, which became numbers 27, 28 and 29 Stephen's Green. Adjoining them around the corner was number 12 Kildare Street. This group of houses, together with their gardens and outbuildings, stood on the site of what is today the main Shelbourne Hotel building.

Luke White is a character worthy of some comment. From humble beginnings as a bookstall keeper near Essex Bridge in Dublin he amassed what has been described as the largest fortune made from trade in Ireland in the eighteenth century. He did it through brilliant innovative manipulation of his own trade as bookseller and through his involvement in a contemporary lottery scheme. His speculative methods outraged some of his more conservative professional colleagues. It is said that in one of those moments of fortuitous impulse, when left with a number of unsold tickets, he bought them himself and won £20,000, a vast sum of money in those days.

White's fortune enabled him to buy Luttrelstown Castle, the former home of the Earl of Carhampton, in whose family it had been since the time of Henry VI. At Luttrelstown, which he re-named Woodlands, White and his wife, Elizabeth de la Maziere, entertained the viceroy and his court. They at first looked with snobbish disdain at the self-made bookseller-turned-gentleman. They had reason to change their fickle minds when they saw the scale of his wealth. He had sufficient good taste to transform the dull castle into a splendid eighteenth-century house and was the envy of many who enjoyed his hospitality. In 1812, Luke White, by then a substantial land and property owner, became Member of Parliament for Leitrim and held the seat until his death in February 1824. His fourth son, Henry White, was created Baron Annaly of Annaly and Rathcline in 1863, and it was he who granted the leasehold interest in the St Stephen's Green properties to the Shelbourne's founder, Martin Burke, in November 1824.

Despite the rapidly rising value of certain south-city property, which certainly included almost anything built on Stephen's Green and Kildare Street, Henry White appeared to have had difficulty finding tenants for the houses built there by his father. A solution presented itself when Martin Burke, then living in Seapoint House in Monkstown, County Dublin, expressed an interest in acquiring the properties with a view to opening a 'quality' hotel.

Mr Burke had quite specific requirements in mind. He needed a range of buildings large enough to be economically viable as a hotel. Because he planned to woo genteel custom his requirements extended to the need for solid, comfortable and serviceable accommodation at a fashionable address. He hoped for a leasehold agreement that was flexible enough to allow him make whatever alterations he deemed necessary to the exterior and interior of the buildings. Henry White, perhaps conscious of the fact that he was risking the disapproval of the affluent residents of the Green by allowing Burke to open a hotel, reined in the Tipperaryman's ambitions rather tightly. The leasehold agreement, dated 27 November 1824, between 'Henry White of Hackettstown, in the County Dublin, Esqre. Lieutenant Colonel in His Majesty's County of Dublin Regiment of Militia' and 'Martin Burke of Seapoint House in the County of Dublin, Gentleman' set down quite strict terms for how the property could be used.

In consideration of a downpayment of £1,000 and the promise of a further £2,000 at a later specified date, and a yearly rent of £300 Martin Burke and his heirs were granted the leasehold interest for 150 years from 1 November 1824. Some of the attached conditions were standard for the time. Mr Burke was required to prevent 'tanners, soap boilers, skinners, distillers, hatters, brewers, and cattle slaughterers' operating within the premises. Burke was also required to finish building, at his own expense, the exterior of one of the houses that would form his new hotel. The most serious contractual sting came at the end: he was required to make no exterior changes whatsoever to the three houses fronting the Green. He was to 'preserve and maintain the windows and hall doors of the said three houses as they at present stand and appear as if they were separate and distinct houses'.

Here lay Mr Burke's dilemma. He had signed a lease, which restricted him to preserving the exteriors of three not especially architecturally distinguished houses. How was he to found a hotel based on three adjoining houses, the fronts of which he was not allowed alter so that they might give the impression to a passer by of a single unified place of business? Burke was little concerned about restrictions on the use of his premises by brewers, distillers, candle makers and tanners but he was very concerned about the way in which the façade of his new hotel presented itself to the world. By 1824, and very well accustomed to the ways of business, he decided his best option was to move ahead, regardless of the dictates of his lease.

Looking at the plain, red brick exterior with its uniform fenestration, Burke found himself pleased by one feature which united the three houses and which he thought he might use to good advantage. This was a wrought-iron balcony, which extended, without division, across the drawing room floor of all three houses. Certainly, by 1850 and perhaps earlier, Burke had thrown caution to the wind and we see, in a drawing from that time, in bold letters across the façade the words 'Shelbourne Hotel'. The legend was well and truly under way.

The name chosen reflected Martin Burke's sense of history but more especially his shrewd sense of business. For a very brief period – possibly while he was waiting for the ink to dry on the lease agreement – the hotel was known simply as 'Burke's'. Now something grander was required and Burke exchanged his family's name on the premises in favour of that of the title of William, second Earl of Shelburne. Taking that name – while also taking the liberty of adding an 'o' – for his new establishment, instantly linked it not just with the fame of the late Lord Shelburne in particular, but with the ascendancy in general. We can only speculate as to the addition of the 'o' in the spelling of the peer's name. It may have been something as simple as the spacing of the lettering on the façade. The Shelbourne remained umbilicaly linked, as it were, to the ascendancy, until, as we shall see later, the emergence of the Ireland of Seán Lemass.

With his premises secured and the name in place, Martin Burke set about the business of organising the interior. The restrictions placed on any exterior alterations did not apply to the interior plan. Here Burke exercised a free hand.

We know from contemporary advertisements that the ground floor contained a combination of the principal public rooms and some bedrooms. There were drawing rooms, dining rooms, a smoking room, and a writing room all on this floor. Burke designed a series of private drawing rooms on the upper floors, which were a major attraction for visiting nobility and gentry up from their country estates for the viceregal 'season'.

The annual move, usually in May, of the viceroy and his court the short distance from Dublin Castle to Phoenix Park, marked the end of the Dublin 'season'. The entire resident members of the ascendancy were expected to attend during the season. Failure to do so was more than mere social death: it was interpreted, especially in the case of a resident nobleman, as disaffection with the ruling order.

Sadly, no major records survive of Martin Burke's first year in business in the hotel but within a year of its opening the Shelbourne was firmly established as a favourite of visitors 'doing the season'. The hub of the social round centred principally on Dublin Castle, which was a short stroll or carriage drive from the Shelbourne's front door.

For many guests the advantage of the Shelbourne was that it enabled them to entertain privately in a public space away from the gaze of inquisitive neighbours and fellow guests. It also allowed them to have all the benefits of a Dublin residence without the attendant costs of maintaining such a household.

When the Shelbourne opened for business, Richard Colley Wellesley, the Marquess Wellesley, had been viceroy for three years. His outspoken pro-Catholic views found great favour in Ireland at a time when Daniel O'Connell's Catholic Association was agitating for reform. His Irish birth further endeared him to a great section of the country. A ditty of the time, however, was more realistic in its interpretation of how the Marquess' hands were tied by duty and loyalty which of necessity lay elsewhere:

Who that hath viewed in his past career
Of hard-earned fame could recognize him here?
Changed as he is in lengthened life's descent
To a mere instrument's mere instrument.

'Mere instrument' Lord Wellesley may have been in the eyes of the street satirists, but in society, he was the very axis upon which Irish upper class social life turned. It was this world principally, which found its way to the newly opened Shelbourne. There was, of course, another world at the very door of the hotel and beyond its comfortably appointed chambers.

Thomas Willis, a philanthropic commentator, carried out an inquiry into the condition of the poor in Dublin in 1845. His report of life in a typical slum dwelling made chilling reading for any Shelbourne guest who may have chanced to peruse it:

> Within this space the food of these wretched beings, such as it is, must be prepared; within this space they must eat and drink; men, women and children must strip, dress, sleep. In cases of illness the calls of nature must be relieved; and when death releases one of the inmates, the corpse must of necessity remain within the room.

The year Willis submitted his report on the urban poor, 1845, is forever fixed in Irish memory. A fungal disease *phytophthora infestans*, commonly called potato blight struck the crop, then the staple diet of a third of the population. The severity of the resulting Great Famine of 1845–1849, touches our subject in the most callous way. The period in question saw the hotel crammed full of ascendancy families seeking escape. Some were oblivious to the misery at their gates; others were conscious only of declining rents, and fearing for their own future. Not all landlords were so calculatingly indifferent. Lord Gort at Lough Cutra Castle in County Galway caused his personal wealth to be considerably reduced in his efforts to help famine victims on his estate. There were others but they were in the minority. It is against this background of upheaval and tragedy that the early history of the Shelbourne Hotel is set.

Within twenty-five years of opening his premises, Martin Burke added the adjoining houses, numbers 30 and 31 Stephen's Green and number 12 Kildare Street to his empire. Failure in so expensive a venture would have ruined him. Dublin, then as now, enjoys failure more that it does success and as Elizabeth Bowen observes in her book, *The Shelbourne Hotel*, 'humours pretension only when it succeeds'. There is no evidence to suggest that the Shelbourne's founder was in any way pretentious. On the contrary, he appears to have been grounded firmly in reality.

In order to oversee the daily running of his venture he moved with his wife Anne into 12 Kildare Street. We find him there when William Makepeace Thackeray made his famous visit to Ireland in 1842. His *Irish Sketch Book* is an invaluable record of pre-famine Ireland. In it he engages his satirical genius to deflate by merciless attack all that displeased or annoyed him. The Shelbourne was spared his savage pen for he seems to have genuinely liked the establishment. From his accommodation, in a small ground-floor room, he drew an interesting sketch of the recently opened hotel and of the city he saw outside its windows.

'A respectable old edifice' is how he described the hotel on first sight. So impressive was Martin Burke's achievement that even Thackeray's piercing eye was deceived. He appeared to be duped by both the recent construction of the buildings, and by the fact that it was not a unified edifice but rather a cluster of houses, presenting what the author saw as a united front on the Green.

He wrote of the hotel as a place 'much frequented by families from the country and where the solitary traveller may likewise find society'. Thackeray was paying six-and-eightpence a day for his stay at the hotel. In return for this sum he received 'a copious breakfast', 'a perpetual luncheon' and 'a plentiful dinner' served at six o'clock. The writer found the hotel 'majestically conducted by clerks and other officers'.

He was accommodated in what he described as 'a queer little room' with a dressing room. Thackeray fans will know this room from his famous description of finding one of its windows propped open, with the aid of a broom handle, after he returned from a stroll. So quaint did he consider the custom that he not only described it in detail but also did a little sketch of it which he included in his book.

> As I came up to it in the street, its appearance made me burst out laughing, very much to the surprise of a ragged cluster of idlers lolling upon the steps next door; and I have drawn it here, not because it is a particularly picturesque or rare kind of window, but because, as I fancy, there is a sort of moral in it. You don't see such windows commonly in respectable English inns – windows leaning gracefully on hearth-brooms for support.

Sadly, there is no sketch of Martin Burke but the landlord is not ignored in the writer's account of his stay at the Shelbourne. Thackeray comments that he did not appear in the hotel during his visit but lived nearby 'where his name may be read inscribed on a brass-plate, like that of any other private gentleman'.

By 1842, Martin Burke was very much a private gentleman and man of affairs. By then, the Shelbourne was but one part of his growing property empire. While maintaining his house in Monkstown he also established himself at 12 Kildare Street from where he conducted his business in the city and kept a watchful eye on the proceedings at the Shelbourne.

He now had an able lieutenant in the form of his eldest son James Milo Burke. James Milo was a barrister, whose principal residence was a Dalkey house called 'Khyber Pass'. He later moved to Queenstown Castle in Dalkey but, like his father, also believed in the benefits attached to a city centre base. This was at 31 Stephen's Green at the Merrion Row end of the hotel. Father and son between them, when in residence, held the Shelbourne in the firm pincer grip of the family.

Martin Burke's Will shows that his property interests in Kingstown date from 1821, three years before he founded the Shelbourne. The arrival of the railway to Kingstown in 1834 created fresh possibilities for property speculators. Plots were bought, quite often from redundant quarry workers who lived in the area. At the forefront of this new suburban development stood the father and son team of Martin and James Milo Burke. The Burkes amassed an impressive property portfolio in the area while at the same time pursing separate careers; Martin in the hotel business and James Milo at the Irish Bar.

Martin Burke became the subject of public notoriety only once in his lifetime. As a substantial property owner he was eligible for jury service. It was an honour he would have happily eschewed. He became unwillingly embroiled in one of the most notorious political trials of the period, that of the Young Ireland leader, Charles Gavan Duffy. The year was 1848.

Gavan Duffy was the editor of *The Nation*, a publication in which he castigated the British establishment for its handling of Irish affairs. Together with several of his Young Ireland associates, he was arraigned for treason. Four separate trials followed at the fourth of which the Attorney General was determined to secure a conviction against him. To this end, the jury was 'packed' with pro-government lackeys. In a later memoir, Gavan Duffy said the jury contained everyone from the Lord Lieutenant's hairdresser to his shoemaker. To provide some semblance of fair play a native Catholic had to be found. To his considerable dismay, the choice fell on Martin Burke. The Shelbourne's owner did not welcome this particular opportunity for public service. It fell to his wife Anne to persuade him otherwise.

The prosecution felt confident that Burke would do as they wished. It was felt his association with the establishment through its patronage of the Shelbourne made him appear a safe pair of hands from the government's viewpoint. Here they felt was a man who would do their bidding. Gavan Duffy himself held the same opinion of Burke but, as he explained in his memoirs some years later, he completely misjudged his man.

The night before the final trial Anne Burke called on Mrs Duffy and informed her that her husband would stand firm for an acquittal. Because of Martin Burke's refusal to compromise on his principles and his wife's determination to see fair play done, Charles Gavan Duffy was acquitted. For taking such a stand, Martin Burke was castigated in the House of Lords on 23 February 1849 during a debate on the Habeas Corpus Act (Ireland) Bill. Lord Brougham intimated that Martin Burke, by insisting on the acquittal, had brought disgrace on the name of the noble lord after whom the Shelbourne had been named. Martin Burke replied through the letters pages of the newspapers, presenting a passionate defence of the rights of jurors.

After his acquittal Charles Gavan Duffy emigrated to Australia and later became Governor of Victoria. Martin Burke became something of a hero to supporters of the nationalist cause. His business at the hotel remained largely unaffected by his pro-nationalist stance or by vitriolic attacks by choleric old peers in the House of Lords. By then the Shelbourne's position as Dublin's premier hotel was unassailable. Even to those who disagreed with Martin Burke's stand at the trial of Gavan Duffy, the Shelbourne had become too much a part of the fabric of their lives to abandon it now.

Martin Burke lived on until January 1863 when he died at the age of 75. The *Dublin Evening Post* marked his passing saying that:

> by honourable industry, Mr Burke had acquired a considerable fortune; and altogether he was one of those practical and public spirited men who have largely contributed to the welfare and improvement of Dublin.

His tomb at Glasnevin Cemetery bears the inscription: 'a fearless Patriot, an independent Juryman, and a true-hearted Irishman.'

He divided his substantial property and investment portfolio in a number of family bequests. His beloved Shelbourne he left to his wife Anne for her lifetime and thereafter directed that it should pass to his son James Milo. Quite soon after his death, Anne and James Milo Burke decided to sell the hotel. Anne was by then too old to continue to bear the burden of running the hotel and James Milo had growing business interests elsewhere. The days of the old hotel, made up of that ramshackle amalgam of St Stephen's Green houses were numbered. An entirely new edifice, the one which stands to this day, was about to rise in its place.

CHAPTER TWO

THE 'NEW' SHELBOURNE

Be gone dull care … make room for mirth and glee.

By the end of February 1866, nothing remained of the hotel where Thackeray encountered the comic broom propping up his bedroom window. Rising in its place was the architectural creation of the distinguished Irish Victorian architect, John McCurdy and his builder Samuel Bolton. His employers, Messrs. Jury, Cotton and Goodman gave their architect carte blanche to execute the work. Only two modest demands were put on him. He was asked to produce a building equal in stature to the great hotels of London and Paris and the work had to be finished within ten months! It seems scarcely credible that the building we look upon today extending 126 feet along the Green, 175 feet down Kildare Street and rising to a great height was completed in just ten months. Three hundred men worked alternate shifts around the clock. Two months were lost in a legal wrangle with the owner of an adjoining property. However, by January 1867 the building was completed.

To the citizens of Dublin it must have seemed a most amazing site. The familiar tall red brick and stucco façade through which patrons access the Shelbourne today began to rise against the Dublin skyline in February 1866. The Burke family had sold their interest in the hotel in December 1865 to the business consortium called Jury, Cotton and Goodman. We shall encounter the characters which made up this somewhat odd partnership at greater length later but for now let us stand across the road from the cleared site of Martin Burke's Shelbourne and witness a new beginning.

McCurdy opted for the Renaissance style for the exterior architecture. The walls are of red brick and the main exterior features are of Portland stone. The principal feature is an entrance porch to which a glass canopy was later added. Two double bay windows rise to the height of the main rooms on the first floor. They were intended for the viewing of public processions. The whole façade is cross-banded in cream painted stucco. A handsome balustrade of a scroll pattern in cast-iron protects the area. Four granite pedestals support full-sized bronze figures of Egyptian princesses and their attendant Nubian slave girls. The four quickly became known by Dublin wags as the last four virgins in Dublin. They are the work of the studio of M.M. Barbezet of Paris. These four ladies holding their torches stand sentinel in front of the hotel and have become its most enduring emblem. In recent years copies of two of the figures have moved indoors where they wistfully but discreetly observe the varied drinking habits of patrons of the Shelbourne Bar.

The new hotel had 15 bedrooms with bathrooms with an additional 25 suites of rooms for guests who wished to entertain more lavishly or merely required greater space. The bedrooms were a generous 23 feet by 17 feet and the adjoining sitting rooms were 29 feet by 23 feet. In those days many patrons travelled with their servants and separate accommodation, which included a basement dining hall, was provided for them. Many also travelled with pets and it was not unusual to find some exotic peer or peeress pitching up at the hotel entrance hall with anything from a monkey to an Irish wolfhound. Most often, however, it was a yapping lap dog making its presence felt to a wary hall porter. Coffee rooms, a smoking room, a billiard room, several dining rooms, a Turkish bath, and a hairdressers added to the comforts offered to the weary traveller. A telegraphy room was considered one of the great innovations of the hotel and it had its own special line. It also had the privilege of issuing its own stamps which consisted of a franking mark bearing the name of the hotel.

The interior decoration was the high Victorian style of the day. Chimney-pieces of richly carved Carrara marble and Valentia slate were set off by rich wall hangings and oriental rugs. Furniture was brought in from London and the rooms were illuminated by gaslight which had first come to Dublin in 1825. By 1881 electricity had taken its place as a source of illumination in the hotel. Interestingly the hotel had only four bathrooms for guests who did not have an en suite room. The eighteenth-century custom of not washing too much lingered on in Victorian Ireland. For those travellers more fastidious about such matters there was endless quantities of water available from the Vartry reservoir which now supplied the hotel and the growing city.

Quality service was the order of the day and it fell to the architect, John McCurdy, to see that the infrastructure supported this in every respect. Today this quiet, genial man, perhaps the greatest hotel architect of his generation and the creator of Dublin's grandest hotel, is, sadly largely forgotten.

John McCurdy was born in Dublin in 1823, just one year before the old Shelbourne Hotel opened its doors. He received his professional training in the office of Frederick Darley, architect to Trinity College, and he eventually succeeded Darley in that post. He went into partnership with William Mansfield Mitchell and practised from Leinster Street as McCurdy and Mitchell. He was president of the Royal Irish Institute of Architects and died at the relatively young age of 61 leaving behind his most enduring legacy, the Shelbourne Hotel building.

The cost of the whole venture to the new partnership of Jury, Cotton and Goodman was enormous for those days. The Burkes received £13,000 for the leasehold interest and the fittings. However an additional £73,000 had to be expended before the doors could be opened to the public.

As is so often the case in Ireland, a legal wrangle or two added to the partners' difficulties. Lord Annaly who owned the reversionary interest in the lease had to give permission for the prohibitive clause of November 1824 to be removed as an impediment to progress. This prevented any alteration being made to the exterior of the old buildings. Now that they had been razed to the ground the absentee Lord requested through his solicitor that the outline demarcation of the old building be marked by vertical lines running up the façade of the new hotel. Builder and architect were incensed by this curious demand.

A compromise was found when the wily Mr Bolton suggested putting the original boundary lines on the roof. They remain there to this very day. An interested party anxious to see where the line of the original houses stood could do so by securing permission for a brisk amble up to the roof space. Lord Annaly's ready consent to the destruction of the houses is seen even to this day by some conservationists as the beginning of the end of Georgian Stephen's Green. Others argue that his decision gave Dublin an architectural gem of another great period though it was something of an architectural cuckoo in a largely symmetrical Georgian square. The partnership's difficulties did not end there. Neighbours too had to be placated. Richard Armstrong, who was in residence at Number 32, was incensed by the building plans. He wrote to William Jury on 21 June 1866 issuing a strong threat:

> Take notice I hereby refer you to a letter which I have this day written to Mr. McCurdy; and I apprise you that I will hold you answerable for all consequences & costs which may be occasioned by any attempt to carry out the plans therein referred to.

Strong words indeed from a potentially litigious neighbour who was by profession a lawyer. However, nothing came of the threat, Mr Armstrong was somehow placated and the building progressed. Indeed within twenty years number 32 was purchased from Armstrong and added to the hotel owners' growing property portfolio.

We must return now to those founders of the new hotel because several members of that family group of Cottons and Jurys will be part of our story from 1867 until the hotel was sold over a hundred years later. One member of the family, Captain Peter Jury, continued his association with the hotel beyond the date of that sale.

The Jury and Cotton families were linked by marriage. William Jury founded the hotel which bore the family name and originally stood on College Green. Charles Cotton was the owner of the Imperial Hotel in Cork and their partner, Christian Goodman had managed the Railway Hotel in Killarney. William Jury's second wife, Margaret, was the sister of Charles Cotton. They had two boys called Charles and Edward. Charles Cotton and his wife had three sons, the eldest of whom, Stephen Fairburn Cotton, we shall encounter later. The Cottons came originally from Scotland but established themselves in the north of England before moving to Ireland. The Jurys hailed from Somerset. A connection with the Imperial Hotel in Belfast brought William to that city before he made his way to Dublin to found Jury's Hotel and the new Shelbourne. His marriage to Margaret Cotton fortified the link between two great Irish hotel dynasties.

The third element of the Shelbourne partnership is one which has posed something of a conundrum for previous historians of the hotel. Christian Goodman appears to have been something of a gentleman adventurer. What is certain is that he had sufficient personal resources to make a one-third capital investment in the new venture. What was uncertain, until the recent discovery of records in the hotel, is the reason for his rather hasty retreat from the business quite soon after it was up and running so successfully. In fact things appeared to go seriously wrong in the partnership by 1871.

Elizabeth Bowen speculates as to the possible reason for Goodman's departure. Did his children, she asks, make too much noise in the rarefied atmosphere of the hotel? Was Mrs Jury too dominant and interfering a personality for his liking? Goodman was in the interesting and unique position as third man in the partnership of also being the hotel's manager. For this he received £300 annually in addition to his share of the profits. He was also allowed to reside with his family free of charge on the hotel premises. All of this was neatly summarised in a memorandum of agreement drawn up just before the hotel opened for business. A mere five years later all was in disarray in the partnership. Mr Goodman was paid £14,500 for his share in the business and he packed his trunks to disappear forever from the Shelbourne. An examination of the hotel records reveals a series of payments to doctors culminating in a payment of £35 for an operation in 1871, the year of his departure. This substantial sum, for those days, indicates the gravity of the operation and the parlous state of Christian Goodman's health. The conveyance of Goodman's share in the business was not effected until 12 April 1886. An unsigned telegram message from the Shelbourne to Stephen F. Cotton in England says 'Since visiting both draft and parchment signed'. Throughout the early months of 1886 a protracted correspondence between Stephen Cotton and his cousin Charles Cotton Jury indicated how anxious they were to buy out Goodman's share. Thus in a letter of 1886, of which only a fragment survives, we witness Stephen Cotton's anxiety over the matter:

> If Goodman refuses to sign anything we might bring an action against him if it was thought wise to do so.

The pressure on the dying Goodman to sell his share back to the other partners began to mount in early April 1886. By 10 April the firm was desperately afraid that Goodman would die before the conveyance was signed. Charles Cotton Jury wrote to his cousin to say Goodman would sign nothing, not even after his mother, Margaret Jury visited the dying man's bed, no doubt lending a new terror to the meaning of death. On 12 April, with the indomitable Margaret Cotton Jury, her financial henchman Alexander Knox McEntire and Goodman's friend Sam Bewley present, Christian Goodman signed over his share of the Shelbourne for the agreed sum of £14,500. That day McEntire wrote to Stephen Cotton in England:

> Mr. Goodman is very ill indeed, I would not be surprised if he died any moment, Dr. Little is in daily attendance and has told Mrs. Goodman that he may drop off suddenly any time.

At no stage was doubt cast over Goodman's management skills. The very year of his departure, 1871, P.B. O'Brien of Gardiner's Hotel, Charing Cross, wrote to the Shelbourne praising Goodman's skills:

> I am glad to hear Goodman is keeping his own –
> he certainly is the best manager I ever saw.

Among Elizabeth Bowen's less fanciful speculations as to the possible reason for Goodman's departure from the Shelbourne is the notion that he very likely came into conflict with the woman who was to become the formidable doyenne and most forceful personality the hotel has known in its history. Margaret Jury may not have been, as Miss Bowen claims on her behalf 'one of the world's great women' but she was certainly the undisputed monarch of all she surveyed within the limited domain of the Shelbourne Hotel.

Margaret Cotton Jury as bride (left) and matriarch (right).

If we rely on a portrait painted in old age for our notion of Mrs Jury's physical presence then the immediate impression we get is one of a formidable matron. Photographs taken of her just after her marriage show a woman of more gentle disposition. Encountering her in old age wearing the full battle dress of Victorian crinoline as she marched along a Shelbourne corridor must have been a daunting experience for staff and visitor alike. She was a woman who had suffered great personal loss. In a very short space of time her husband, teenage son, brother and mother all died.

Once in place at the Shelbourne, Margaret Jury ruled the hotel with a rod of iron. Her word and hers alone was law. This is all understandable when one considers her background. She was first of all born into the hotel business. There was no aspect of the trade this impressive woman did not know. Then, upon marrying, she further consolidated her ties with the hotel world.

While her husband and brother chose to adopt the role of 'sleeping partners' in the venture and spend their days on their collective business affairs and their lives in splendid isolation in suburban mansions, Mrs Jury was at the very coalface of life at the Shelbourne. It was she who prepared for the printer the following notice which advertised the services of the new hotel:

> *Messrs. Jury, Cotton & Goodman beg respectfully to inform the Nobility, Gentry and Families visiting Dublin, that the Shelbourne Hotel will be open for their reception on the day of January, 1867.*
>
> *The Hotel has been rebuilt from the foundation, on the newest and most improved principle, and will be found one of the most complete in its appointments in Europe … It contains, on the ground floor, a magnificent Coffee Room, a Ladies' Coffee Room, a Table d'Hôte Room, and a General Reading Room … a Billiard Room, a* Hair-dressing Room and a Telegraph Office, *which two latter features will, no doubt, be highly convenient and of special advantage … The situation of the Hotel is the most delightful in the city. Its aspect is southerly, and from each window a splendid view of the Dublin and Wicklow mountains is obtained, whilst it has the advantage of possessing for the use of its visitors the large and beautifully laid out pleasure grounds of the Green; as respects the Railways the situation is also more central than that of any other Hotel in Dublin.*
>
> *The* cuisine *will accord with the other arrangements of the establishment.*
>
> *There will be a Table d'Hôte each day …*
>
> *N.B. The Continental Languages spoken by the Manager and Waiters.*

When Christian Goodman handed over the keys to Margaret Jury the business was flourishing and in excellent order. In the first full year of trading, from February 1868 to February 1869, hotel receipts were

£22,318/4/5. Outgoings in the same period were considerable indicating that trade was very brisk indeed. In the first six months, simple provisions such as meat, eggs, fish, butter and bread cost the hotel £4,460. Noble quantities of the finest clarets and brandies were imported directly. The hotel archive holds an invoice from G. Sayer of Cognac for five Hogsheads of fine pale cognac costing just over £54. A cellar book lists the great wines of the period at prices that seem absurd in modern times. Chateau Mouton Rothschild at four shillings a bottle and Chateau d' Yquem at five shillings a bottle. What is particularly striking is the vast consumption of the finest Havana cigars and Turkish cigarettes. The hotel housed a speciality shop where smokers' requisites could be purchased. The heady smell of tobacco posed no annoyance in those less politically correct times.

In the first years of the hotel's accounts the specific duties of staff or their number are not listed separately. We know, however, that the average monthly wages for the total number of men employed in the hotel was £60.

The account books tell us that the goodwill established by Martin Burke marched on with the apparent ease of a prosperous omen. The hotel's finances went from strength to strength. Brisk and successful trading was aided by a solid investment portfolio, which included Dublin and country property and judicious stockmarket investment. Margaret Jury saw to every detail of that portfolio alongside the management of the hotel. Her dealings with lawyers, accountants, architects, engineers and the all-male world of Dublin business is truly remarkable when one considers that at this time a woman was not allowed to vote, control her own bank account or sign documents while her husband was still alive.

The position of chattel did not suit Mrs Jury. Under her severe scrutiny bad debts to the hotel were few in those early years of business. Those that are recorded indicate that her lenience extended principally to senior members of the aristocracy and the military. Thus under 'Bad and Doubtful Debts' we see entered in the ledger for 1877 Sir C. Nugent owing over £35, a Captain Baker £6 and in 1888 the Irish Rugby Football Club are down for just over £8. The following year Lady Rosse is listed for a trifling seven shillings and beside her Colonel H.B. Bernard for the more substantial sum of £47. Mrs Jury was not hesitant when it came to threatening legal action on reticent debtors. In April 1884 this stinging reminder was issued to Lord Clanmorris:

> We beg to call your Lordship's attention to the amount due to this Hotel, as per a/c enclosed.
>
> The applications for payment which have been sent by us hitherto do not appear to have come under your notice.

Lord Rossmore received a similar letter requesting the payment of £50 due on his account. There was a tendency amongst peers of the realm to show a certain disdain towards tradespeople's bills. Those foolish enough to put the Shelbourne in that category usually had occasion to revise their mistaken opinion. Mrs Jury would have none of it. Lord Clanmorris's account, along with those of other foolhardy peers, was sent to a lawyer for collection.

The hotel records show that a stern letter from Mrs Jury was usually enough to send most patrons scurrying for their cheque books. After her departure, as we shall see later, 'bad and unrecoverable debts' became something of a plague for the Shelbourne management for many years to come.

The hotel was not immune to personal injuries claims even in those days. When a Mrs Hughes threatened such an action in January 1884, the ever vigilant financial adviser, Alexander Knox McEntire, entered the fray to defend the hotel's best interests. He wrote to Mrs Jury on 14 January:

> It would be well at this time to collect all the facts of the case and put them in detail in the form of a letter in order that some opinion of a local character from an experienced quarter might be obtained as to the probable extent of the monetary liability of the proprietors of the Hotel ... Such opinion should be had from a leading lawyer, accustomed from experience to the assessment of damages by Dublin jurors.

Increasingly the affairs of the hotel were concentrated solely through Margaret Jury's hands. After the dissolution of the Goodman partnership, William Jury's health began to fail. He died in Bristol on 16 August 1872. His wife Margaret and his two sons, Charles Cotton Jury and Edward Scott Jury inherited his share of the hotel. Edward died five years after his father on 19 November 1877 and as a final blow Margaret Jury's brother also died suddenly.

Between these devastating family bereavements she fought off a legal challenge by the children of her husband's first marriage who tried to lay claim to Edward's shares in the hotel. She won that case convincingly. Finally, together with her son Charles who reached the age of 21 on 1 October 1876, and her nephew, Stephen Fairburn Cotton, who had inherited his father's shares, Margaret Cotton Jury was firmly in place to guide the Shelbourne through to the very doorstep of the new century.

Because of its long association with British army officers stationed in Ireland, the Shelbourne sometimes got caught up in the turmoil which these men were sent to Ireland to keep in check. We shall encounter times ahead when the hotel will play a more direct role in these often violent events but for now, in those early days of the new hotel, all was relatively quiet within its precincts. The attempted Fenian rising of 1867 had little impact on the hotel save for the increased number of top brass British military personnel coming and going. The land war of 1879 to 1882 had a more serious impact on the hotel's principal customers – the landed gentry. The growth of nationalist sentiment demanded that the British government do something immediate, particularly about that most sensitive of issues – the land question.

The Land Acts essentially made possible the transfer of ownership from landlord to tenant. In 1870 the legislation made customary tenant right enforceable at law and provided compensation for disturbance. By 1881 the 'Three Fs' – right of free sale, judicial power to fix rents, conversion of ordinary tenancies to fixed tenancies – were all in place. By 1885 the Land Commission was allowed to lend to tenants so that they could purchase their holdings from landlords. By the end of the nineteenth century the landlord class – the Shelbourne's best customers – were an endangered species; by the beginning of the twentieth century they were practically extinct. Agrarian relations in Ireland were so appallingly unsatisfactory that it could be no other way.

All of this impacted upon the Shelbourne in a number of ways. More and more landed families were spending time in Dublin and using the hotel as their base. In addition quite a number of former landlords' sons were moving to Dublin-based professions, especially the Irish Bar. Many of them, including Elizabeth Bowen's barrister father, Henry Cole Bowen, were using the Shelbourne as a Dublin social base.

Stephen Cotton, son and heir.

These families were, with rare exceptions, staunch unionists. Their landed interest had preponderated in the old Irish parliament. The majority of the Protestant landlord class now felt their interests better preserved in the imperial parliament in London than by any concession offered to Home Rule in Ireland. One can imagine the likely effects of the objectives of constitutional nationalists hotly debated over port and cigars by landed gentlemen after the ladies had withdrawn from table at the Shelbourne. The approach of Mr Butt and later Mr Parnell to the 'transfiguring vagueness' as Home Rule was once dubbed, must have provided endless evenings of lively debate in the heavily smoke-filled rooms of the hotel. What indignant outrage must have been expressed at the Reform Act of 1884 which enfranchised the rural householder. From 1885 onward no landlord stood a chance of being returned at an election in Ireland unless he was a Home Ruler. By 1898 the landlord class had lost control of local government and by the beginning of the twentieth century, even as local administrators, the gentry were a disappearing and endangered species. The novelist George A. Birmingham effectively described such a man gazing down from a window of the 'big house' over a large tract of land and sighing 'it is mine no longer'.

The 1912 edition of *Burke's Landed Gentry of Ireland* records many of the older families still resident in their original family seats. Several landlords decided to stay on and many made valuable contributions to public life. Speaking in the House of Commons, Colonel Saunderson, a southern unionist, said 'in our own native land – we are Irishmen as much as the tenants are – we love our nation as much as they do'. The ascendancy did indeed, almost to a man love Ireland; it was the native Irish they had difficulty with.

George Moore.

As the old order was being swept away, the Shelbourne, together with a few institutions such as the Royal Dublin Society, and the Kildare Street Club became increasingly important focal points for the new dispossessed. The Shelbourne remained the most valued Dublin gathering place for this class and would remain so until the new order was firmly in place. It would be at least 1957 before the landed class, which had patronised it since its doors first opened, would find a diminished role in the financial well-being of the Shelbourne. As an institution the hotel developed an uncanny sense of moving sensibly with the times.

The novelist George Moore (1852–1933), himself from a family of County Mayo gentry, chronicled aspects of Mrs Jury's Shelbourne on a number of occasions. We find in *Parnell and His Land,* his rather bitingly astringent picture of how the disgruntled 'stranded' gentry looked out from the Kildare Street Club on the changing scene around them. The neighbouring club was in some ways an annex to the hotel:

> This club is a sort of oyster-bed into which all the eldest sons of the landed gentry fall as a matter of course. There they remain spending their days, drinking sherry and cursing Gladstone in a sort of dialect, a dead language which the larva-like stupidity of the club has preserved. The green banners of the League are passing, the cries of a new Ireland awaken the dormant air, the oysters rush to their window – they stand there open mouthed, real pantomime oysters, and from the corner of Frederick Street a group of young girls watch them in silent admiration.

Moore, in somewhat mellower and more benevolent mood, gives us a most lyrical portrait of the situation of the Shelbourne. In *Ave*, the first volume of his trilogy *Hail and Farewell*, we find him in reflective mood concerning the outlook of the hotel where he is staying:

> All about the square the old brick houses stood sunning themselves, and I could see a chimney-stack steeped in rich shadow, touched with light, and beyond it, and under it, upon an illuminated wall, the direct outline of a gable; and at the end of the streets the mountains appeared, veiled in haze, delicate and refined as The Countess Cathleen. A town wandering between mountain and sea, I said as I stood before my glass shaving...

To Moore we owe the most complete *fin de siècle* portrait of what the hotel was like at the height of its glorious days before the gathering storm of the Great War. The hotel Moore describes in his novel, *A Drama in Muslin*, though set during the Dublin season of 1882 changed little in the thirty-one years before the beginning of World War I.

'We shall be' exclaims Mrs Barton, mother of the book's heroine, Alice, 'very comfortable at the Shelbourne; we shall meet all the people in Dublin there, and we can have private rooms to give dinner parties'. Mrs Barton used the Shelbourne as the base from which to launch her daughters on the uncertain world of husband-hunting while 'doing the season'. It is in the hotel's drawing-room, that the shy Alice encounters the cynical and gossipy Mr Harding, who tells the impressionable west of Ireland debutante that under the very roof where her mamma has billeted her, 'All the events of life are accomplished'. For 'life in the Shelbourne', the chatterbox opines, 'is a thing in itself and a thing to be studied'.

The year in which Moore set *A Drama in Muslin*, 1882, saw the customers of the Shelbourne shocked by the grimmer reality of life outside its precincts. On 6 May, Lord Frederick Cavendish the newly arrived Chief Secretary for Ireland and his Under-Secretary, T.H. Burke, were stabbed to death while walking in the Phoenix Park. The Invincibles, an extremist Fenian group, claimed responsibility. Both Irish and British public opinion was horrified by the brutality of the murders.

Surgical knives were used in the attack. Burke had been the intended target; Cavendish had only just arrived in Ireland and his murderers were unaware of his identity. As a result of the murders Gladstone was forced to maintain Coercion in Ireland at a time when it was about to be dropped. A deeply depressed Parnell briefly considered resigning from parliament. The continuing uncertainty over Gladstone's Home Rule plans left a particularly dark mood in place amongst the Shelbourne's patrons especially after the general election of 1885 and the Prime Minister's renewed efforts for Home Rule. The hotel records for the period show a not inconsiderable drop in business. County families stayed on their estates fearing something akin to revolution. Fashionable overseas society cancelled their travel plans for Ireland and the Shelbourne's public rooms echoed rather forlornly in the absence of jollification.

Tariff.

1st OCTOBER to 31st MAY.

Apartments.

(Including **Baths,** *Light and Attendance.)*

Single Bedrooms .... from 6/- to 15/- per night
Single Bedrooms, with Private Bath and Toilet, 16/6 to 20/-
Double and Two-bedded Rooms 14/6 to 20/- per night
Double Bedroom, with Private Bath, from £1 5s. od. to 32/- per night
Double Bedroom, Dressing Room, and Private Bath and Toilet,
2 persons .... from £1 15 o per night
3 persons .... ,, £2 o o per night
Sitting Rooms .... 15/- to 30/- per day
Sitting Room and Single Bedroom, *en suite,* from 34/- to 44/- per day
Do. and Double .... from 39/- to 48/- per day

An additional charge of 6/- is made for each Supplementary Bed.
An extra charge for Apartments is made to all Visitors who do not Board at the Hotel.

These Prices are subject to alteration during Punchestown, Spring Show, and other special occasions.

A Shelbourne tariff card.

Yet even with business thus depressed we find the hotel's owners, especially Mrs Jury, planning to extend and improve the premises. She badgered her fellow directors in detailed letters about the need to spend more money on the hotel. In 1883 she became obsessed with the need for the Shelbourne to have a passenger lift. Protracted negotiations got underway in 1883 for the purchase of the adjoining house to the east, number 32 Stephen's Green. The house was originally the property of Lord de Montalt, and passed on his death in 1777 to his brother Sir Cornwallis Maude, created Baron de Montalt in 1785 and Viscount Hawarden in 1791. Subsequently the house was the home of the Attorney General, William Saurin and from 1863 of Richard Armstrong, Sergeant-at-Law. It was from this gentleman's family that the house was eventually purchased and it was that same man who attempted to stir up trouble for the new venture in 1866. The house contains some well executed stucco work, principally on the first floor. It has been attributed to the Dublin stucco-worker, Edward Robbins.

Margaret Jury wished to acquire the house to prevent any building work adjoining the hotel at the rear. She also wished to extend the number of bedrooms and reception rooms. To this effect the adjoining house, number 33, was also acquired and many years later number 34, thus giving the Shelbourne the whole block from Kildare Street to what is presently known as Huguenot House. The Shelbourne also purchased number 26 Stephen's Green, giving it a hold on the other side of Kildare Street. Mrs Jury set about furnishing the additional rooms and organising discreet interconnecting passages which even to this day confuse the patron wandering the breadth of the great range of buildings.

Mrs Jury had exacting standards and she required the same high standards of her staff. If they lived up to her expectations they could expect her unwavering loyalty and support in return. When a Mr Purcell of Monkstown mistakenly blamed the Shelbourne staff when some articles of his went missing but were later found by their owner, Mrs Jury jumped to the defence of her staff:

> We have no doubt that you will at once see … that a few words in a letter which could be read to the servants referred to acknowledging the discovery, by you, of the missing articles, would be just and proper.

In 1891, the year of Parnell's death, Margaret Jury decided to vacate her suburban residence, Airfield House, Dundrum, and move permanently into the Shelbourne. Staff, family and no doubt many regular patrons were visibly shaken by the old lady's resolute decision to install herself on the premises. In old age she was a difficult quantity to manage. Neither her senses nor her energies had been dulled by the passage of time. Changing times, however, made her outlook more resolute and some would say tyrannical. Despite advancing age she was still in sufficient possession of her faculties to strike an excellent deal with the hotel partnership for the contents of her house which she now sold on to the company. A melange of Victorian and Edwardian furniture, some of which is still to be found throughout the hotel was off-loaded for the handsome price of just over £313. With the installation of the furniture came the attendant installation of the old lady's hands-on dictatorship, something which caused considerable friction throughout the hotel. Neither family, employee or friend dared tell the mistress her time was up. It seemed neither war, natural disaster nor act of God could move the immovable. Margaret Cotton Jury would remain doyenne of the Shelbourne until she saw fit to make her own move.

This led to a major family crisis and endangered the hotel's very existence. By mid-May 1894, it is quite clear the family was at its wits' end over Mater's presence in the hotel. Her nephew, Stephen Cotton, had withdrawn to England to live in Sydenham. Her son, Charles Jury, was, poor man, still on hand in Dublin and bearing the brunt of all comers' complaints about his mother's meddling. His health began to fail and he pleaded with his cousin Stephen to intervene.

Stephen Cotton contacted the only person he felt he could burden with the difficult request he was now about to make. For many years the most intimate Shelbourne and family business finances were handled by the trusted financial adviser Alexander Knox McEntire of Foster Place, Dublin. McEntire was the inventor of the bank passbook which registered clients' daily balances. He was an extremely accomplished and shrewd accountant and devoted to the financial affairs of the Shelbourne. He was across every aspect of the hotel's business.

In a letter dated 18 May 1894, Stephen Cotton wrote to McEntire to inform him that 'a crisis has come in the affairs of the Shelbourne and unless we are able to arrange matters amicably I think we will be forced to sell the hotel'. He went on to tell McEntire that his cousin Charles Jury had been staying with him and had made it quite clear that unless his mother, Margaret, was persuaded to retire, the hotel would be lost to the family. Charles and Stephen, in private conference in London, had made up their minds that Margaret must go. They took the unusual step of asking poor Mr McEntire to be the message carrier to the old lady. Stephen made a final plea in his letter to McEntire: 'Unless Mrs Jury can see that this is the proper course to take I see no other course open but to sell the hotel,' and he adds the sting in the tail 'as representing half the capital I must have influence in the decision'.

The entrance hall in the late nineteenth century.

There was now to be no turning back, a clear course was set. McEntire was told a manager must be found and since it was quite clear to the family that no manager on earth would satisfy the 'old lady of the Shelbourne', she must cede way or the hotel was to go under the hammer. Neither history nor legend records the old lady's reaction or when exactly the news was broken to her. She assigned her interest in the hotel to her son and nephew on 23 July 1896. One imagines a haughty yet dignified disdain coupled with her own hard-nosed sense of reality prevailing on her as she was asked to bid farewell to her beloved Shelbourne. She took leave of her staff with quiet dignity and sailed with her son Charles for England.

Professional to the very end, her last task was to sit down and write in alphabetical order 'Instructions from Jury & Cotton Shelbourne Hotel Dublin to Geo. R. Olden'. Mr Olden, whom we shall soon meet more formally in the next chapter, was the hotel's new manager.

'Coal', the old lady instructed, 'should be used sparingly on mild days in the public rooms throughout the house and fires should be slacked when the weather allowed'. 'Complaints', she instructed, 'must be investigated at once, personally by the manager and set right and if affecting general management must be reported to the firm'. 'Dress: Manager must wear frock coat and dark tie when on duty'. 'Porters: Porters must never go out without managers' permission'. 'Bathrooms: Must not be let as bedrooms except under great pressure'. There were separate instructions for Horse Show Week and for Punchestown Races and for a hundred different things from electric light to dispensing drinks to telling staff to turn off lights in corridors. She was leaving her beloved Shelbourne in good hands but she was determined that her stamp would still be on it. All of this was two years before Cézar Ritz opened the doors of the Paris establishment bearing his name.

How saddened Margaret Cotton Jury must have been to read in the English press in April 1900 of the Shelbourne's honourable mention in relation to the imminent visit of Queen Victoria:

> At the exclusive Shelbourne, they are turning everybody away, including guests hitherto in possession, in order to make room for a large special party; so that you see the Shelbourne has got on in the world since the days when Thackeray, staying there, used to find his bed-room window, in the front of the house, propped open by a casual broom-handle.

Margaret Cotton Jury did not survive long in exile. She died on 5 January 1904, just about outliving her queen. Her Will left the bulk of her estate to her family and there were several bequests to Dublin charities. She also left bequests to two Shelbourne porters, one of £50 and the other of £30. She stipulated that they were to receive the money only if still in the employ of the hotel. Margaret Cotton Jury remained a Shelbourne woman to the end. After her death her family's direct connection with the Shelbourne was to continue for another fifty-six years. They were to be amongst the most interesting years for the hotel, which emerged, like the country whose capital it so elegantly adorned, a greatly changed place.

CHAPTER THREE

AVE MR OLDEN

It seems that they want someone learned and well-born to function in buttons and braid at The Shelbourne!

Arriving at the Shelbourne, along with the new century was its first manager in the true sense of that term. With the death of Margaret Cotton Jury, on 5 January 1904, and the departure of her son Charles for residence in England, the hotel was now in the sole charge of G.R.F. Olden whose task it was to guide the establishment into the new century. In a sense, George Olden's presence at the helm was a continuum of the Cotton-Jury hegemony. He was a relative of the Jury's. Despite the kinship with the owners, Olden was very much his own man and the hotel's survival, in a rapidly changing Ireland, owed much to his management style. He came to the Shelbourne on 9 November 1896 to apprentice himself to the departing shade of Mrs Jury. It fell to him to guide the Shelbourne through some of its most interesting and its most troubled times.

Two factors combined to dampen the heralding in of the twentieth century in Dublin. The Boer War was at its height and the lists of Irish officers and men, dead or missing in South Africa, filled the daily newspapers. Big house and humble cottage alike were giving up their sons to a conflict those at home scarcely understood. In 1899 New Year's Eve fell on a Sunday. This also lessened the impact of the celebrations. No state ball was held at Dublin Castle. Private parties were less strident than they might otherwise have been. The Shelbourne, however, had a full house and liberal quantities of champagne, mostly Bollinger 1892 and 1893, priced at six shillings a bottle, were consumed.

Mr Olden's first ten years at the Shelbourne coincided with the full blaze of the reign of King Edward VII. In 1885, as Prince of Wales, Edward visited Ireland with the Princess of Wales. In Cork the royal couple were booed and pelted with rotten vegetables. In Dublin the Kildare Street and Sackville Clubs held a ball in their honour. The couple returned in 1903 and 1904 as Edward VII and Queen Alexandra and again in 1907 when the highlight of their visit was the news of the theft of the 'Irish Crown Jewels'. It occurred four days before the royal yacht docked in Dublin. The so-called 'Crown Jewels' were, in fact, the insignia of the Order of Saint Patrick worn by the viceroy and grand master. They were of exquisite quality and ornamented with diamonds, emeralds and other precious stones, mounted on gold and silver. Their estimated value was around £50,000.

The jewels were kept in a safe in the Office of Arms in Dublin Castle. The safe had not been forced open and this led the police to suspect an insider job. Suspicion fell on one particular Castle staff member whose open homosexuality and taste for high living made him stand out from his more staid colleagues. He was known to have had a relationship with a handsome army officer who was based in Dublin Castle. Both men knew Lord Ronald Gower, a rakish English homosexual and uncle of the King's brother-in-law, the Duke of Argyll. The speculation at the time was that even though the King was furious about the theft, he feared a homosexual scandal involving a relative of the royal family. A large reward was offered but no trace of the jewels was ever uncovered. Rumours of their sighting around the world still surface from time to time.

Interior photographed by William Lawrence, late nineteenth century.

The theft of his Irish Crown Jewels, coupled with the hurling of vegetable missiles in Cork, did little to shake the affable Edward out of his fondness for Ireland. His munificence beamed forth on an island where he could get comfortably drunk, enjoy excellent game shooting as well as the favours of certain suitable women. All of this augured well for the Shelbourne. As Elizabeth Bowen put it: 'The receptionists' books coruscated with noble names'. Between the royal visit of 1907 and the Easter Rising of 1916 the hotel began to adapt to a changing world. Its first guest lift was installed in the lobby in 1907. Sadly it involved changing the configuration of Mr McCurdy's rather splendid staircase. The imposing central flight was moved to the left to accommodate the lift cage and entrance doors at lobby level. The vestibule or mezzanine landing, designed as a winter garden with bubbling fountain also had to yield to the new contraption. It became a popular area for taking tea and even today remains one of the quieter and least-used oases of the bustling hotel. Gone too are its murals of pastoral scenes which were painted on the arched panels long ago.

The citizens of Dublin came in their droves to witness the new lift in operation. Its open cage afforded a view of guests ascending to the upper floors or making their way down to dine or depart from the front lobby. A pair of bronze statuettes on plinths remained in place, flanking the lift entrance, as they had once flanked the now displaced central flight of steps. These patient ladies quietly observed every arrival and departure at the Shelbourne since 1867 until they were replaced mid-century by a pair of electrified candelabra which are still *in situ*.

Mr Olden was a stickler for detail and kept the most meticulous records of the minutiae of the operation of the hotel. In the year of his arrival, 1896, the hotel's receipts totalled £29,171. Under his management, receipts rose to £46,374 by 1907. That year saw the addition of another floor to the Kildare Street wing. This was the first and only major structural change to McCurdy's exterior design for the hotel. The addition of a glass awning, extending beyond McCurdy's entrance porch was the only other change.

Business was greatly helped in 1907 by the opening of the Great Irish International Exhibition at Ballsbridge. It was opened by the Lord-Lieutenant, Lord Aberdeen, and attended by the King and Queen. It attracted record numbers of visitors to Dublin. That year the Shelbourne received 49,671 guests with receipts per 100 guests averaging £93. At this time a single bedroom ranged from four shillings to eight shillings and six pence per night. A double room cost from eight shillings to twelve shillings. Suites started at fifteen shillings. Luncheon cost three shillings and six pence and dinner cost five shillings. To have a fire in one's room cost two shillings a day or a shilling if lit only in the evening.

Part of Mr Olden's grand scheme for the hotel was to develop the tourist trade. He felt the Shelbourne stood in danger of being dominated by its regular patrons and that overseas visitors would feel excluded by this cosy arrangement. Olden engaged in an advertising campaign in England and in the United States and from the beginning of the century we see the guest registers containing a great number of American names, especially from April to September. August remained the preserve of the Irish county set who essentially took over the hotel during the Dublin Horse Show at the Royal Dublin Society. This event remained, until very recent times, the single most important event in the hotel's calendar.

In 1904 the Manager's salary was £48 per month. This included an annual allowance of £76 for house rental. Then, as now, managers preferred not to live on the premises. Most front of house staff settled in for long tenures in their jobs but there was a high turnover of head chefs in the kitchen. Between April 1903 and March 1911 six came and went. In 1904, forty members of staff lived on the premises or in nearby Kildare Street. The hotel had its own coachman who drove patrons in a brougham. The age of the motor car had yet to impinge on the Shelbourne. In 1908 the coachman was paid eighteen shillings a week and his food was reckoned at an additional ten shillings. The running of the brougham, which included, horses, insurance, stabling, feed, and farrier costs was estimated at £178 a year. The hotel made a profit on the venture of £32. Staff, or servants as they were still called at this time, seemed happy in the Shelbourne. In a clipping kept by Mr Olden, from *The Caterer And Hotel-Keepers' Gazette,* he takes note of the situation in New York:

> In one sense, hotel-keepers, restaurateurs and others welcome the alleged 'hard times' which have struck New York and other big American cities because for once in a while they have no difficulty in getting servants. It is no longer necessary to meet the incoming alien immigrant and assure him or her of a happy home with little work and plenty of wages. The servants themselves recognise that the tide of prosperity is not at the flood and there is unanimous agreement that the menials generally are less exacting in the terms which they command from the complacent master.

Such an attitude did not prevail in Dublin under George Olden's leadership at the Shelbourne. He had much more than 'the servant problem' to worry about.

Maintenance was a constant drain on hotel finances. Between 1903 and 1928 the exterior was painted seven times. In June 1925 a new laundry was installed at a cost of £1,606. Up to that point sending laundry out was costing the hotel about £1,000 per annum, most of which was charged to patrons using the service. New bathrooms and WCs were added throughout the hotel in 1910. To take a bath cost one shilling.

Under Olden's management the fusty Victorian interior soft furnishings were gradually replaced and the hotel took on, within agreed limits, the feeling of a twentieth century hotel. The management was, as it had always been, willing to embrace change. It had welcomed and taken advantage of all sorts of technological innovation as soon as they were available such as the telephones which rang out in lobby and halls. The brougham was replaced by the motor car and the Shelbourne suddenly seemed an altogether busier place.

As business continued to improve the hotel staff numbers increased. The *Evening Mail* carried this amusing ditty in 1913 as to the type of person who might find employment at the Shelbourne:

Ex-officer or public school boy wanted for position as Hall Porter in Dublin hotel. One who is not afraid to turn his hand to work.
Your Harrovian culture is that which equips
You to sort and distribute the travellers' grips;
Useful your knowledge of Homer and Livy
In urging those so and so bell-hops to chivy.
Applied mathematics will aid you dictate
That number fifteen must be wakened at eight …
It seems that they want someone learned and well-born
To function in buttons and braid at the Shelbourne!

In 1913 the hotel staff were not members of a trades union. It was the year of Ireland's best remembered labour dispute, known as the Great Dublin Lockout. It began in August when a number of employers led by William Martin Murphy attempted to force workers to withdraw from membership of the Irish Transport and General Workers' Union. By September some 20,000 workers were on strike or 'locked out'. Labour leaders James Larkin and James Connolly were arrested for sedition. Two workers were killed when police confronted demonstrating workers in Sackville Street. The strikers lacked the resources to prolong the dispute and by January 1914 most had returned to work on whatever conditions they could best obtain. For the months of the strike guest numbers at the hotel were considerably reduced – in some months nearly halved. Figures for the years of the Great War show a considerable increase in business.

It was Mr Olden's intention to retire in 1914, after eighteen years of service. Duty bade him stay. He was to steer the hotel through a general strike, a world war, a rebellion and a civil war, before dying on vacation in England. In a notebook Olden kept during his time as manager he makes observations – often in the form of a single phrase accompanied by a date – on events which impacted on hotel business. Thus in 1912: 'Bad Season and the Duke of Fife died'; 1913: 'Death of the King of Greece and Larkin's Strike'; 1914: 'Home Rule Bill' and 'The Great War'.

When war was declared in August 1914, Olden decided he would not abandon the hotel in its hour of need. Its need was great indeed because war had barely been declared when the police arrived at the hotel to arrest the majority of the male waiting staff. Ever since the Cotton-Jurys took over the hotel a tradition had been established of hiring German and Austrian waiting staff. How strange the sight must have been of waiters dressed in tail coats and white tie being shunted in an undignified manner into Black Marias in front of the Shelbourne. Leading the group was the head waiter, a German called Francis. He had given many years of faithful service to the hotel. It is said he was so long at the Shelbourne that he believed himself to be Irish. George Olden was galvanised into action and secured the temporary release of his men pending their further internment which occurred later. Junior Irish waiting staff were pressed into action and thus did an emergency create a new tradition in the Shelbourne. From 1914 on, the majority of the waiting staff were recruited in Ireland. By 1919 the German head waiter was replaced by a Frenchman, Monsieur Charmartin who was paid £1/12 a week. The hotel also began to employ women to wait on table, a function which had always been a strictly male preserve in the Shelbourne.

In 1914, Ireland, as part of the United Kingdom, was expected to play its part in the war effort. Any threat of rebellion in the country was defused at the outbreak of war when both John Redmond and Edward Carson pledged their support to the British imperial war effort. Such support from the Unionist leader was understandable but Redmond met with some resistance amongst his nationalist supporters. However his call for support for Catholic Belgium was heeded by over 270,000 Irishmen or 40 per cent of the adult male population. This figure does not take into account the emigrant Irish who joined up in England and elsewhere or the numbers working in munitions factories. Thirty thousand Irishmen lost their lives. On the first two days of the Battle of the Somme, which began on 1 July 1916, the 36th Ulster Division lost over 5,000 men. Such sacrifice was seen by Unionist leaders as demonstrable loyalty to the idea of the Union.

In Ireland Maude Gonne's notion of England's moment of difficulty being Ireland's opportunity was put into action in the form of the Republican Rising of Easter 1916.

The details of the Rising are well known. What is less well known is the Shelbourne's connection to the events of Easter Week 1916. The Rising was planned for Easter Sunday, 23 April, but the failure to secure German support, amongst other reasons, caused the Dublin Volunteer leader, Eoin MacNeill to call it off. Patrick Pearse, the schoolmaster poet who commanded the Dublin Volunteers and James Connolly, the labour leader, who commanded the Citizen Army, decided to go ahead as planned.

Volunteer and Citizen Army units took over strategic buildings in the capital and ran up various forms of republican emblems on flag poles. A proclamation was read from the steps of the General Post Office and fighting continued until the insurgents surrendered on 29 April.

The Shelbourne had its usual contingent of racing folk in residence on the evening of Sunday, 23 April. The Fairyhouse Races were the principal attraction of the Easter season. The War added an additional cast of military personnel to the already crowded Shelbourne stage. Lieutenant Colonel A.E. Woods was down from his Enniskillen base, two members of the Jameson family from Drogheda were staying. On Monday, Sir Robert and Lady Anderson arrived with one servant, as did Captain Kirk of the South Irish Horse and Colonel Lowry from Pomeroy. By the evening of Easter Monday when news of the Rebellion reached the Shelbourne the register was closed and no further guest entries were made until Sunday, 30 April when one finds only six guests in residence. Business was marginally curtailed only until mid-May when guests began returning to the hotel. The figures show a decrease of only 150 guests from the same period the previous year.

Throughout the period of the Rising, George Olden and his staff remained at their posts. Olden moved into the hotel and directed operations from room 82. On Easter Monday itself most of the senior British officers posted in Dublin were attending Fairyhouse Races. Confused rumours circulated on the racecourse. Returning to the Shelbourne, the residents heard that Dublin Castle had been attacked by six members of the Citizen Army who walked up to the gate and shot a policeman dead. Several Shelbourne patrons got caught up in the fighting. Lord Dunsany and his chauffeur were both shot and wounded near the Four Courts. The insurgents took Dunsany to Jervis Street Hospital. A nun who attended his wounds ignored the bullets whizzing past through the window and viewed the insurgents with disdain as 'the nasty little things'.

British troops depart the Shelbourne down Kildare Street.

Just down the street from the Shelbourne, the Kildare Street Club came under mistaken attack. There was much to-ing and fro-ing between the Club and the Shelbourne. Lord Fermoy, anxious to see the progress of things stood at the Club's bay window overlooking Trinity's cricket crease. A British army sniper thought he was directing the insurgent's fire against the soldiers who had taken up a position on the roof of a college building in the afternoon. He took a pot shot, narrowly missing the inquisitive peer. When the mistake was discovered an apology was sent to the club and the members responded by sending club servants out with trays of food for the soldiers. Lord Donoughmore, a regular Shelbourne patron, received a flesh wound as he came near the hotel in his soft-topped motor car.

What was especially shocking for the ascendancy patrons of the Shelbourne was the sight of one of their own class strutting about the Green in the uniform of a colonel of the rebel volunteers. The officer was Countess Constance Markievicz, the daughter of an Anglo-Irish, County Sligo family, the Goore-Booths of Lissadel. In 1887, she was presented to Queen Victoria at court in London and attended two separate London seasons, earning the appellation 'the new Irish beauty'. She studied art at the Slade School of Art in London and also in Paris where she met her future husband Count Casimir Dunin-Markievicz who came from a Polish aristocratic family. She joined Sinn Féin in 1908, took part in Larkin's 1913 Lockout and by the time of the Rising was convinced of the justification of armed resistance to British rule in Ireland. She served as second in command at the College of Surgeons, just across the Green from the Shelbourne.

We have a very clear eyewitness account of the situation outside the Shelbourne on that Easter Monday from the writer James Stephens. He was passing the hotel on his way from the National Gallery where he then worked. The 'rebel Countess' had organised her troops about the Green and placed a roadblock or barricade near the hotel. Stephens approached from Merrion Row:

> I came to the barricade. As I reached it and stood by the Shelbourne Hotel, which it faced, a loud cry came from the Park. The gates opened and three men ran out. Two of them held rifles with fixed bayonets. The third gripped a heavy revolver in his fist. They ran towards a motor car which had just turned the corner, and halted it. The men with bayonets took positions instantly on either side of the car. The man with the revolver saluted, and I heard him begging the occupants to pardon him, and directing them to dismount. A man and a woman got down. They were again saluted and requested to return to the sidewalk. They did so.

James Stephens made his way towards one of the rebels and asked the meaning of all this:

> He replied collectedly enough in speech, but with that ramble and errancy clouding his eyes. 'We have taken the city, we are expecting an attack from the military at any moment, and those people', he indicated knots of men, women and children clustered towards the end of the Green, 'won't go home for me. We have the Post Office, and the railways, and the Castle. We have all the city. We have everything'.

This account by Stephens was written down almost immediately after he witnessed the events outside the Shelbourne. It captures several elements corroborated by other eyewitness accounts of how Countess Markiewicz's men conducted themselves. She was most insistent that her troops behave with the utmost civility towards ordinary citizens going about the business on that warm and sunny, holiday Monday. There is also the sense of elated confusion in the young rebels account of how his comrades had 'taken the city'. They had taken certain strategic locations, the most symbolic of which was the General Post Office. They might indeed have taken the Shelbourne itself. It is no doubt one of those apocryphal stories beloved of Dubliners but it is said that the Countess, on passing the Shelbourne with her men, looked up, and, seeing its vast size, dismissed the idea and made her way instead to the more manageable Royal College of Surgeons. There she billeted her men. Another such story has it that the Countess and the British forces ranged against her organised a cease fire every day at lunchtime so that the Shelbourne staff could feed the ducks in the Green who had been mightily discommoded by all the hullabaloo. For a long time, as Seán O'Casey remarked, 'Easter Week became the Year One in Irish history and Irish life'. It was also a seminal date in the Shelbourne's history.

The hotel owners, depending as they did on the ascendancy and the British establishment in Ireland for the success of their venture, remained singularly loyal to the Crown during the Easter Rebellion. However, some members of the staff did not. Many years later it emerged that one hotel porter made regular forays up to the rooftop from where he signalled the movement of troops within the hotel to the Countesses' forces across the Green. We shall meet him again much later in our story.

Given the level of disturbance outside the hotel it is a remarkable testament to George Olden's management and to the dedication of his staff that life inside carried on almost as normal. On Easter Monday it was traditional for large numbers to come to the hotel to take tea. The ladies especially enjoyed the airing of their newly acquired Easter millinery. Even the presence of a substantial barricade outside the hotel did not deter the eager patrons. Elegant ladies were seen scrambling over upturned carts in order to make their way to the Shelbourne drawing room. By 4.30 p.m. the room was full to capacity for the afternoon ritual. Occasional sniper fire rang out across the Green. It took all Mr Olden's efforts to keep inquisitive ladies away from the windows. His efforts were more carefully heeded when a sniper's bullet neatly pruned a bunch of roses from their standing position atop one matron's hat. Waiters scurried to gather up tea trays and remove the somewhat shaken patrons to the safety of the Writing and Reading Room at the rear of the hotel (this room is now the Horseshoe Bar). By early evening, the racing set started to file into the lobby looking for dinner. Each had his own story of the day's events in the city. Many were so inebriated that they had no notion of the Rebellion until sobriety broke upon them the following day.

Captain Andrews (left) officer in charge of the Shelbourne garrison with Colonel Madden.

On Tuesday afternoon, forty soldiers, under the command of a Captain Andrews, were sent to garrison the hotel. This made it a legitimate target for the rebels across the Green and the Shelbourne came under regular fire for the remainder of the week. The place took on a claustrophobic air. The windows were sandbagged and shuttered. The great entrance door was barricaded. A skeleton staff operated the hotel's services and titled guests were drafted in to act as waiters.

The ladies' curiosity with the action outside the hotel abated once corpses began to appear on the pavement outside. Many guests took to sleeping on mattresses in the corridors. By the end of the week provisions began to run low. Some stout soul braved the gunfire to attempt to restock the kitchen. By Wednesday Mr Olden had given orders to allow the injured and the dead to be taken into the hotel irrespective of which side they were on. Thus did young men who had over the past days fired gunshots relentlessly at the façade of the hotel come to be its guests and have their wounds tended by women whose very existence they threatened.

On Saturday 29 April the insurgents surrendered. Many of those fighting in Stephen's Green with Countess Markievicz wished to continue fighting. She urged them not to. She also stopped one of her men shooting an unarmed British officer who came to the College of Surgeons after the surrender was declared. By a curious coincidence the officer accepting the surrender was her kinsman by marriage, Captain Henry de Courcy-Wheeler. She refused his offer to take her in his car and said she would walk with her men. How strange the sight must have been of this aristocratic woman in rebel garb moving away from the Green on her way to her condemned cell in Dublin Castle. Her death sentence was later commuted and she was sent to prison in England. Many of her own class, including Lord Powerscourt, expressed the wish that she should be shot. She was released in the general amnesty of June 1917 and died in 1927 in a public ward of a Dublin hospital.

The Rising left 64 insurgents, 132 Crown forces and 230 civilians dead. Much of the city centre was devastated by heavy artillery fire. As the British soldiers marched to take the surrender of the General Post Office they were cheered on by the public who stood watching. Attitudes changed overnight when the leaders of the Rising were executed. The 'terrible beauty' of Yeats's phrase exacted a high price. There was particular resentment among ordinary citizens about the reckless shooting of civilians by soldiers during the rebellion. There was public outcry at the shooting of the pacifist Francis Sheehy-Skeffington by

Captain John Bowen-Colthurst, a relative of Elizabeth Bowen's. Bowen-Colthurst was in command at Portobello Barracks where Sheehy-Skeffington was taken after his arrest. The Captain also shot an unarmed man and two boys in central Dublin. His actions were put down to shell-shock suffered in the Great War.

A Cantrell and Cochrane van with a Red Cross flag removing a corpse from the 'trenches' opposite. The abandoned car opposite to the hotel had, at that stage, been there for a week.

It was to the War that people's thoughts returned after the Rising. As soon as hostilities ended in Dublin, the Shelbourne staff began taking down the sandbags and receiving guests. Many came to Dublin for the sad business of arranging funerals. The list of Shelbourne patrons who had lost family in the Great War grew at an alarming rate. Mr Olden wrote to all of his patrons who had been bereaved. They included the family of Lord De Freyne and his half-brother George French, Lord Kenmare who lost a son, the family of Lord Desmond FitzGerald and Lord Carbery whose uncle was killed.

The increase in the number of military personnel brought increased prosperity to the Shelbourne. Military men on leave often headed to Dublin where food was in plentiful supply. There were certain restrictions in place which hotels were obliged to observe and Shelbourne menus from the period carried notices saying that meat and bread were limited to small quantities per person. Because so many of the hotel's patrons were the owners of landed estates, the Shelbourne found itself the grateful recipient of generous quantities of game and other meat. This allowed the kitchen a delicate way around the awkward rationing restrictions. The menus also show quite brilliant vegetarian inventions by the French chefs, and fish, considered penitents' food in Ireland at the time, began to appear on the hotel's menus with great regularity. Gross receipts for the period of the Great War were up and reached an all time high in August 1919. The figure was £7,409 which would stand as the highest earnings the hotel would achieve until 1923.

The barricades running from the Shelbourne porch to the chains bordering the opposite side of the road.

The Shelbourne combined its Christmas celebrations for 1918 with a victory dinner. The chefs drew up a special menu which had dishes associated with the victorious Allies. 'Petite Marmite à la Française, Crème Japonaise, Filet de Sole A l'Americaine', sat side by side with 'Jambon de Limerick avec Sauce Italienne'. Plum Pudding with Brandy Sauce and

Mince Pies appeared as the only token gesture towards conventional Christmas fare on that memorable 25 December on Stephen's Green. The hotel had a particularly busy Christmas and New Year. Dublin Castle hosted a victory ball on New Year's Eve. It was one of the last great glittering events for Anglo-Irish and Castle Catholics alike.

That December was especially memorable for other reasons. In the General Election held in December, Sinn Féin won 73 out of the 105 Irish seats at Westminster, a resounding success which saw the virtual collapse of the old National Party and the establishment, in January 1919, of a parliament or Dáil in Dublin.

The year 1920 was a troubled one for the Shelbourne. Big Jim Larkin's 1913 lockout had little or no impact on the hotel but a strike of 1920 saw all staff march out of the premises leaving Olden no option but to close down the hotel. It remained shut for most of April, May and June with only the assistant manager, Mr Powell, in residence. He had the lonely task of patrolling the empty reception rooms and corridors of McCurdy's great building. His only company were the wild cats who took over the kitchen in the absence of the hot-headed French chefs who kept them at bay.

A further indication that great change was underway was the fact that chauffeurs went on strike. Lady Alice Howard was shocked when her driver was nearly hauled from her car in Fitzwilliam Square when he refused to join his striking colleagues. George Olden kept the hotel's owners informed by letter of the progress of the strike. In a letter dated 10 February 1920 he had already expressed his views to the owners about rising wage costs:

> I can quite understand your concern in the alarming increase in wages which of course includes the salaries of Green Cheque as well as manual workers and still the Daily Press educating the workers & rubbing in the fact that the Sovereign is value for only half or less than pre war. Many argue that they are underpaid.

He first mentioned the strike in a communication of 13 April 1920:

> We woke up this morning to see the announcement of a general Strike throughout Ireland – no trains, no steamers, no trams or cabs, and at 10 o'c. all our male

staff downed tools and congregated outside the front door to see the women out – the girls mainly didn't want to go and they all worked hard to get their rooms ready and then left by 11 o'c. The loyalists would have remained but the risk was too great with the whole city idle and we sent them all away except the chef and the two women in the plate pantry, who refuse to leave. We then organised among the visitors 12 volunteer waiters and served cold lunch. We could see the Green black with people. Punchestown races are postponed till Wednesday and Thursday, but the general opinion is that if the protest has no effect the strike will continue.

Valentine's Day 1919 – Martin Carolan, waiter, (right) signed for his wages of £1/0/9, on this day.

Olden informed the hotel's owners that their average 'mens' wage bill for a week in 'pre-war pre-strike days' was £57. After the nine-week strike it rose to £105 per week. The 'womens' wage bill, he observed, increased by £30 a week. He added that, with the departure of two particular staff members, the power of the union was weakened in the hotel. He felt confident, therefore, that he could resist any further demands for increased wages.

The vigorous guerrilla war against the British, which commenced in January 1919 and was undertaken by what had become known as the Irish Republican Army, continued with growing ferocity. Sinn Féin had become the voice of nationalist dissent after their victory in the 1918 election gave a fresh momentum to the aspirations of separatists in Ireland. The conflict known as 'the Anglo-Irish War' lasted until a truce was signed in December 1921. It was followed by a bitter civil war after the Dáil's ratification of the Peace Treaty with Britain in January 1922. The treaty was signed in London on 6 December 1921. It created the Irish Free State as a self-governing dominion within the British Commonwealth. Throughout these crises, the Shelbourne remained under the calm guidance of George Olden who was determined that politics and war would not shake the now ageing lady on the Green.

Olden could see that the old order was doomed and that the Shelbourne, if it was to survive in the new Ireland, must accommodate the emerging regime. However, vestigial links to the world of Anglo-Ireland would remain part of the Shelbourne's fabric for some time to come, but it would not be until the late 1950s that the Shelbourne became a place where the native Irish would feel at home.

CHAPTER FOUR

THE OLD ORDER CHANGES

Things are desperate here … So far thank God we have escaped, but there is no knowing.

In the course of its history the Shelbourne grew steadily accustomed to playing its part in momentous historical events. It was accustomed to having its calm daily routine turned on its head to facilitate whatever was happening in the world outside its doors. Garrisoned by the British in 1916, it also played host to the new army of Ireland during the Civil War in 1922. George Olden was informed by letter that certain units of the army would use the hotel as a base on Stephen's Green. Initially the whole building was not used and staff and the general public were allowed access. Olden was notified that if he 'attempted to give notice outside' he would be arrested immediately. The progress of the Civil War, as it touched the hotel, was reported in letters by Olden to Stephen Cotton and Charles Jury in England. Hostilities began on 28 June 1922 and ended with the declaration of a unilateral ceasefire on 30 April 1923.

Olden first reported the attack by Free State troops on the headquarters of the anti-treaty Irregulars in the Four Courts building. The war, as it affected the Shelbourne directly, lasted no longer than a couple of weeks. By August 1922 the pro-Treaty side had taken control of most urban areas and calm and customers returned again to the Shelbourne.

Olden's first communication was written in April and in it he attempts to judge the outcome of things:

> Things are approaching a climax, I think, and meetings are held today to try and arrive at a 'truce' … at the back of my brainbox I feel things will turn out well in the end, tho' it is sad to feel how much we are losing by the upset. The Hibernian [hotel] was attacked last night. We have a few 'refugees' here from the [Kildare Street] Club nearby and from the West of Ireland – numbers are 27.

He wrote again on 28 June when he had a better feel for what was happening:

> We are back again to rebellion days … at 4 o'c. this morning artillery and machine gun firing started by the Free State troops against the Four Courts. As I write, 3 o'c. it is still going on … the rebels to divert troops from the Four Courts have started seizing hotels …
>
> The Prov. Govt. have again sent us a guard of 9 men … It is just our luck, about 80 people booked on Monday for The Builders Conference which I dare say will be all knocked on the head.
>
> All telephones suspended and now telegrams stopping.

The next day, 28 June, Olden wrote again to say that the Irregulars had seized the neighbouring University Club at 17 Stephen's Green and snipers were seen on many adjoining roof tops. He heard a rumour that the Shelbourne was a target for the anti-Treaty forces. Plain clothes policemen were stationed in the entrance hall and all the guests, with the exception of 47 journalists covering the war, left the hotel. 'We are trying to keep cheerful', he wrote, 'and keeping out of the danger zone.'

On 29 June tones of desperation and worry sound in his letter:

> Things are desperate here ... the 4 Courts in flames after an explosion ... the Hammam Hotel was taken last night, and just now the Gresham was taken by the Repubs.
>
> So far thank God we have escaped, but there is no knowing.

The following day 30 June, he allays the owner's fears in a brief telegram: 'All right here. Under protection.'

The ever practical and businesslike Olden told his employers that the garrison, which he said was 'very friendly', had agreed to pay its food bill. He also told them if a truce was arranged he felt he should fly the Irish tricolour over the hotel and he made enquiries about the price of a twelve by six foot flag. The Union flag is very often seen in photographs and illustrations of the hotel at this time. There were times when it presence outside the hotel marked an official government presence within. This was the case in May 1916 when the Royal Commission appointed by the British Government to inquire into the Easter Rising sat in the Shelbourne. Chaired by Lord Hardinge the Commission heard evidence from a host of witnesses before passing the blame for the administration's bungling of things onto the shoulders of Augustine Birrell, Chief Secretary of Ireland.

Now, in 1922, the Shelbourne played host to its most historic meeting. From February to May 1922 the hotel was the place where work was undertaken on the drafting of a Constitution for the Free State.

Theoretically the drafting committee was under the chairmanship of Michael Collins but in practice that role was taken by Darrell Figgis. Collins had hoped to construct a republican document acceptable to the anti-Treaty side by circumventing some unacceptable aspects of the Treaty. The British would have none of it and forced Collins' hand. Under the new Constitution, government and authority derived from the people. However executive authority was vested in the King but exercised by the Executive Council. Lloyd George found it to be too republican a document for his taste and republicans in Ireland found it totally unacceptable. By the time the Free State Constitution was replaced in 1937, 41 of its 83 articles had been amended.

Apart from the charismatic Collins the other members of the drafting committee were: R.J.P. Mortished, E.M. Stephens, P.J. O'Toole, John O'Byrne, Professor Alfred O'Rahilly, James Douglas, James Murnahan, James MacNeill and C.J. France. The Irish Free State Constitution derived from one of three drafts drawn up in a first floor room of the Shelbourne, room 112, over looking the Green. The event was commemorated in the hotel by the renaming of room 112 as The Constitution Room. The first person outside the Committee to receive a copy of the Draft Constitution was the Shelbourne's manager, George Olden. The Draft was ratified by the Dáil in December 1922.

It was a time of change and the Shelbourne changed with it. Mr Olden did get the opportunity to fly the newly purchased tricolour from the mast. Inside the hotel the khaki of the British officers' uniforms was replaced by the olive-green of the Irish officers who now frequented the old hotel alongside the remaining de-colonising mandarins from Dublin Castle. For Christmas 1922, with Ireland in the full flush of independence, the Shelbourne not only flew the flag but it also made a stab at gaelcising its menus. The Christmas menu was decorated with a border of shamrocks, written in a Gaelic script and contained a first course 'Filet de Sole Baile Aithe Cliach' [sic].

In the decade after independence, the hotel continued to be the haunt of the Anglo-Irish but many of the successful Catholic bourgeoisie, lawyers, politicians, doctors, began to frequent the Shelbourne. Socially they took their lead from the Protestant old order. What other model did they have? Dress, manners, social events were still dictated by those supporters of the old dispensation. Much of their world remained intact, the Horse Show, various race meetings, the Kildare Street Club, Trinity College, the Protestant schools like St Columba's for boys and Alexandra College for girls. Sacred to the memory of how things used to be, was the Shelbourne Hotel. Any patron who frequented the hotel in pre-independence days found it little changed in the years immediately following independence. It was the emergence of the petit bourgeoisie from rural Ireland which wrought the greatest change on the fabric of urban social life and on the Shelbourne itself. But this change was not really evident in the Shelbourne until the late 1950s.

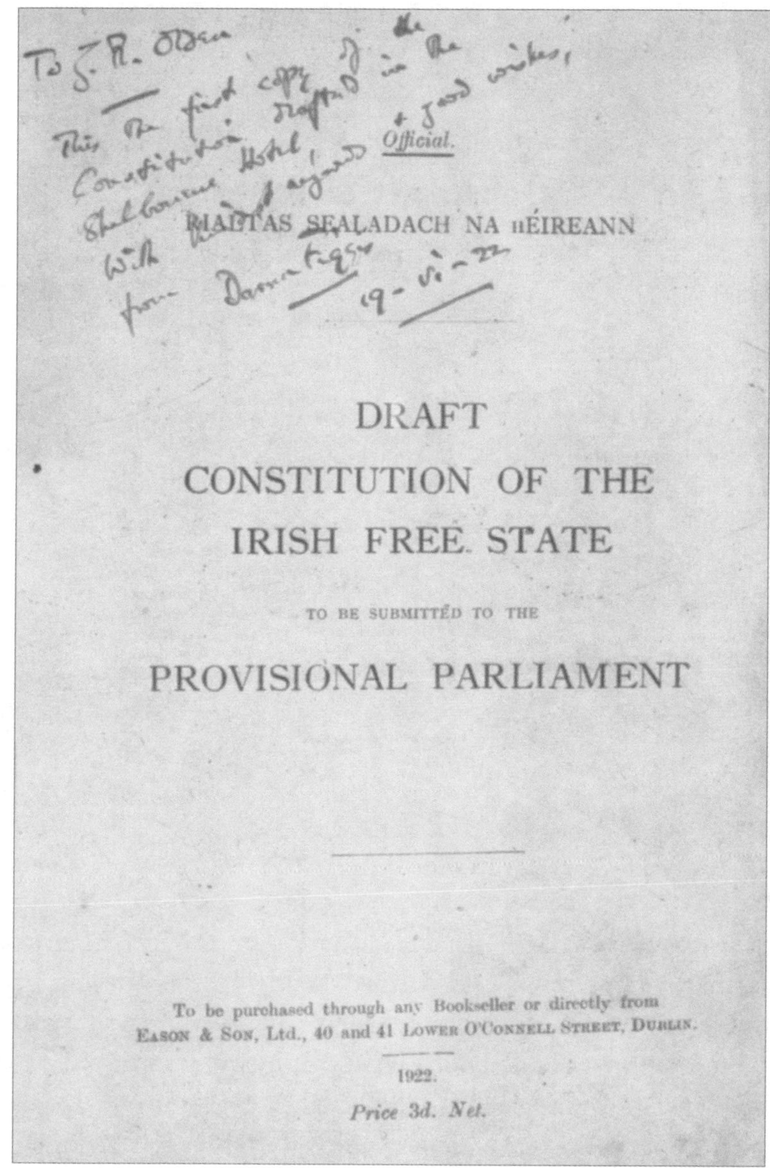

Official.

RIALTAS SEALADACH NA hÉIREANN

DRAFT
CONSTITUTION OF THE
IRISH FREE STATE

TO BE SUBMITTED TO THE

PROVISIONAL PARLIAMENT

To be purchased through any Bookseller or directly from
EASON & SON, Ltd., 40 and 41 LOWER O'CONNELL STREET, DUBLIN.

1922.

Price 3d. Net.

Free State Constitution (1922) presented to Shelbourne Manager, George Olden.

'What would Dublin do without the Shelbourne?' Oliver St John Gogarty asks in *As I was going down Sackville Street.* Gogarty, author, sportsman, wit and medical man, had consulting rooms in a house nearby the hotel and now incorporated into it. He was immortalised by his friend, James Joyce, as Buck Mulligan in *Ulysses.* Joyce too makes several references to the Shelbourne in his writing, most memorably, perhaps, in *Ulysses.* It is in the Shelbourne that Leopold Bloom buys from Mrs Miriam Dandrade some old wraps and black underwear.

W. T. Cosgrove, President of the Executive Council, 1922, with a group of visiting tourist officials.

Eight years after the Shelbourne made its appearance in *Ulysses*, its most famous manager, George Olden, died suddenly, not in his beloved Shelbourne but while on holiday at Holyhead. The year was 1930. The management of the hotel fell once again to a member of the Jury family. Colonel E.C. Jury, grandson of William and Margaret Jury, was called on to come over from England. He was born in Dublin but brought up in England where he became a career army man. He was an experienced professional soldier having entered the army as a teenager and risen to command his regiment, the 18th Royal Hussars, in India after World War I. He held the post of managing director of the Shelbourne until 1947. The seventeen years of the Colonel's reign were characterised by his application of military precision to the running of the hotel's affairs. It did not always work as an effective way of running things. Indeed Colonel Jury often found himself in conflict with a staff who had become much more unionised since the days of Mr Olden. The wages books for the period show ever increasing numbers of staff paying union dues. Any conflict between the Colonel and his staff was kept well hidden from the customers and guests. The thing that did not change was what Elizabeth Bowen called 'the hotel's primitive human core'.

The Gate Theatre moved into its new premises in 1930 and in the early years after the move two young guest actors cut quite a dash in the Shelbourne. They were James Mason and a very young Orson Wells. The latter became a more frequent visitor to the hotel when his stock rose in later years.

If being a Protestant was no impediment to accessing the Shelbourne, it did, however, have disadvantages elsewhere in Ireland. In Mayo, Miss Dunbar Harrison was refused a county library appointment because it was alleged she knew little or no Irish and because she was a Protestant. When she pointed out that she was a Gaelic scholar, though of the Protestant faith, the government demanded she be appointed. The 'Protestant Shelbourne' gained indirectly from a triumphalist Catholic event in 1932 when Dublin hosted the Eucharistic Congress. The pomp and circumstance attending the visit of the Papal legate, Cardinal Lorenzo Laurie, had a vicarious benefit for the Shelbourne. His arrival in Dublin on 20 June meant the Shelbourne was booked solid for a week.

Later that year the Dáil was dissolved and de Valera and Fianna Fáil came to power, winning power again in an election which followed quickly in January 1933. Politics of the period was characterised by the presence of the fascist group, the National Guard, under the leadership of General Eoin O'Duffy. Politics, fascist or otherwise, continued to impinge very little on the Shelbourne throughout the 1930s. A more serious blow was the opening, in August 1935, of the first American-style cocktail bar in the cellar of The Royal Hibernian Hotel. Situated on nearby Dawson Street, this hotel was the Shelbourne's greatest rival. It would be another decade before the Shelbourne made a move to outdo the Hibernian in the cocktail bar stakes.

Tourism boomed in the mid-1930s. In 1935, foreign visitors spent over four million pounds in Ireland. In the late 1930s some guests arriving at the Shelbourne made their journey to Ireland by air. In 1931 Aer Lingus was established and by 1935 it had bought its first aeroplane. It carried five passengers and a pilot on its inaugural flight to Bristol in May. By the end of the 1930s a new international airport had been established at Collinstown, Co Dublin.

The Free State Constitution of 1922 was superseded by the Constitution of 1937. The Free State became Éire on 29 December and on 25 June the following year, Douglas Hyde was installed as the first President of Ireland.

Hyde, a quiet unassuming Gaelic scholar, had been a patron of the Shelbourne for many years and continued to frequent the hotel after he became President.

In 1939 the reality of war, or 'The Emergency', as it was known in Ireland was brought home to any Shelbourne patron who cared to look out of the windows to the Green. Trenches were being dug in the ornamental gardens and soon the even harsher reality of rationing would hit the population. Longstay guests arriving at the Shelbourne from Great Britain or elsewhere were required to register with the Civic Guard, a move which Colonel Jury deeply resented at the Shelbourne. In time of war, as in peace, the Colonel's loyalty to the Crown never wavered.

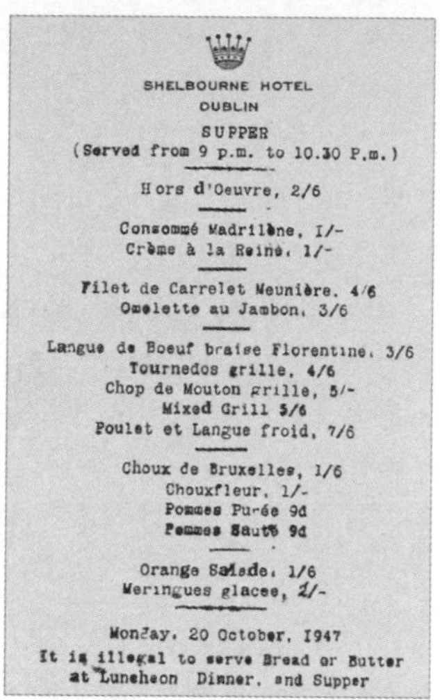

SHELBOURNE HOTEL
DUBLIN
SUPPER
(Served from 9 p.m. to 10.30 P.m.)

Hors d'Oeuvre, 2/6

Consommé Madrilène, 1/-
Crème à la Reine, 1/-

Filet de Carrelet Meunière. 4/6
Omelette au Jambon, 3/6

Langue de Boeuf braise Florentine, 3/6
Tournedos grille, 4/6
Chop de Mouton grille, 5/-
Mixed Grill 5/6
Poulet et Langue froid, 7/6

Choux de Bruxelles, 1/6
Chouxfleur, 1/-
Pommes Purée 9d
Pommes Sauté 9d

Orange Salade, 1/6
Meringues glacee, 1/-

Monday, 20 October, 1947
It is illegal to serve Bread or Butter at Luncheon Dinner, and Supper

CHAPTER FIVE

A STATE OF EMERGENCY

I humped my knapsack and strode off along the river.
At least I knew where the Shelbourne lay.

The outbreak of World War II altered the cast at the Shelbourne and expanded it enormously. The year-end figures for visitors staying during the Emergency show an average annual increase of about six thousand per year, starting at 19,333 in 1940 and rising to 61,496 in 1946. It was a period which began to change the hotel irrevocably, from a discreet residential enclave to an artery through which the life of the city flowed. Many of the regulars joined the armed forces and were seen less frequently. Some of them never returned. Herr Vogelsang, who had been the lounge waiter for many years was interned at the Curragh for the duration of the war. When it was over, he came back to the hotel and resumed his duties as though he had been absent for no more than a few weeks.

Neutrality during the Emergency did not absolve Ireland from all the discomforts and restrictions of wartime. Imports like tea, sugar, petrol and coal were extremely scarce and Seán Lemass, then Minister for Supplies, introduced rationing. Innovative country folk made ersatz tea from hawthorn leaves and the rare blooms in many a greenhouse, hothouse and orangery were turfed out to make space for a personal supply of tobacco. Private motoring became a thing of the past as battered horse-drawn vehicles were recommissioned and Dublin teemed with bicycles.

Dubliners still danced at the Shelbourne, Metropole, Gresham and Clery's, arriving on two wheels instead of four. Formal dress was *de rigeur*. Gentlemen in white tie tucked their tails up beneath them on the saddle and wore bicycle clips and their partners perched on the crossbar holding the long skirts of their evening dresses up out of the mud. Nevertheless, the city was attractive to war-jaded visitors. Steak and ham had become memories in Britain and even butter, though rationed, was far more easily available in Ireland.

Arrivals sailing into Dublin found a sharp contrast to the austerity that they had left behind. The city lights, shining across the water were a heartening sight after the blackout. The city seemed safe and cheerful, far from the uncertainties of the Blitz. Forgotten indulgences could be savoured at the well-furnished tables of places like the Shelbourne. Access, however, was not easy. Travel was severely curtailed. Diplomats and journalists could move freely between the two countries and military personnel and factory workers employed in Britain were granted permits for visits home. Others found permits difficult to obtain.

A trip to Dublin offered an escape from the stringencies of rationing for visitors from the north and the city offered many enticements for rural families from the south too. Since the national petrol shortage had restricted excursions from home to the range of a pony and trap, country dwellers had been starved of company. Big houses and farms all over the country were limping on under the management of stranded women, who had to adapt to new regulations such as Seán Lemass's compulsory tillage programme, while worrying about the husbands, sons and brothers away on active service. A few days up in town offered them a welcome respite from anxiety and isolation. In the past, the company frequenting the Shelbourne had been quite predictable. The wartime traffic brought more variety.

Serving officers returning home from overseas would make for the hotel on Stephen's Green. Its familiarity was reassuring, even if the old standards sometimes became eroded by the exigencies of the Emergency. Churchill's cousin, Anita Leslie, recalled a brief visit during 1945 in her wartime autobiography *A Story Half Told*. She had been excused from driving an ambulance in the French Army to come home and visit her sick mother. The uniforms of belligerent nations were not allowed in neutral Ireland, so military personnel changed into mufti on the boat. Others, like Anita Leslie, de-militarised themselves by simply donning a mackintosh and stowing their service cap in a pocket before disembarking:

> In heavy fog we reached the Dublin docks. The boat was hours late and there was no transport of any sort. The usual horse drawn cabs had gone to bed. People with luggage stood around disconsolate. I humped my knapsack and strode off along the river. At least I knew where the Shelbourne lay.

Booking in at midnight, exhausted, she closed the windows of her room and tried to sleep but was assailed by freakish nightmares of a grinding sawmill and animals nesting in her hair and frolicking on the bed. Waking with daylight she felt something stirring under the eiderdown. She peered cautiously beneath it to find an immense rat curled upon her knees. The animal had been trapped in thc room when she locked herself in for the night. A heap of sawdust beneath the wainscot, where the rodent had tried to gnaw his way to freedom, explained the steady grinding that had disturbed her night's rest. The porter, summoned to deal with the intruder, explained that the kitchens were being repainted and the displaced rats were running riot all over the building. The inconvenience would only be temporary. Presumably they would return to their old quarters once the renovations were completed. One wonders if the feasting carnivores up in the dining room would have relished their steaks and ham quite so much if they had been aware of the unofficial residents below stairs.

A regular visitor to the Shelbourne during the war was the writer, Elizabeth Bowen. Her memoir, *The Shelbourne Hotel*, was published in

1951. Cyril Connolly had suggested the project some years before and her wartime visits to the hotel would certainly have increased her familiarity with it. In 1941 she completed *Bowen's Court.* In hindsight it seems like an elegy for a vanishing world. In less than twenty years her house would have vanished without trace as the old solidities of Anglo-Ireland grew more elusive. Throughout the remaining war years she worked intermittently on her novel, *The Heat of The Day,* but her unpublished writing during that period had a more ambivalent content and explains her unusual freedom of movement at that time.

Elizabeth Bowen.

While publicly expressing support for Irish neutrality she also did her bit for the Allied war effort, working as an air raid warden in London and occupying her London home in Regent's Park until it was bombed in 1944. Her family background and her marriage to Alan Cameron, an Englishman (described once by her friend May Sarton as 'rather blimpish') made these patriotic activities not only understandable but inevitable. For many like her the war had resuscitated the ever-dormant Anglo-Irish paradox. Ireland's landed gentry often felt a conflict of loyalties. Ireland had nurtured them well but they owed their status, indeed their very invention, to imperialism.

In her twenties, Elizabeth Bowen had lived through the Troubles. Friends, relations and neighbours had been victims of terrorism, burned out of their homes in a purge that made refugees of former gentry. Big house families had turned their backs on the blackened shells of their homes to build new lives in the colonies or the middle class enclaves of mainland Britain. It is not surprising that Elizabeth Bowen sometimes sensed an alien and menacing world lying in wait outside the walls of

Bowen's Court. Like George Bernard Shaw, she and her peers often felt English when in Ireland and Irish when in England, a duality which Seán O'Faolain memorably summed up as 'heart-cloven and split-minded'.

The ambiguities of Bowen's allegiances led her to proposing her services as a British Intelligence operative in Ireland, an arrangement not entirely devoid of financial and pragmatic advantages. In 1940, writing to Virginia Woolf she explained:

> I think I told you I had asked the Ministry of Information if I could do any work, which I felt was wanted in Ireland. On Saturday morning I had a letter from them saying yes, they did want me to go. Now it has come to the point I have rather a feeling of dismay and of not wanting to leave this country. I am to see Harold Nicholson on Thursday and go to Ireland on Friday night next – If there's to be an invasion of Ireland I hope it may be while I'm there – which I don't mean frivolously – but if anything happens to England while I'm in Ireland I shall wish I'd never left.

The secret reports which she compiled from then on, confiding to nobody in Ireland about her mission, were sent to Lord Cranborne who described their content as 'sensible and well-balanced' and passed them on to Churchill. Her brief was to ascertain Irish attitudes to the war, especially in connection with British use of the Treaty Ports in the south and west of the country. Some communiqués are tinged with a colonial asperity, quite absent from her published work. In one improbable information gathering exercise she spent a cosy afternoon with the uncompromising prelate John Charles McQuaid, Archbishop of Dublin, enthusing about the work of the Municipal School of Cookery.

A more valuable source of information, who interested her deeply was James Dillon who, although sometimes accused of Fascist tendencies, wanted Ireland to give more tangible aid to the Allies. In February 1942, he was expelled from Fine Gael for stating this belief publicly. At the conclusion of the war, Dillon was responsible for preventing Adolf Mahr, the Austrian-born Nazi from returning to his post as Director of Ireland's National Museum. Mahr had spent the war in Berlin where he effectively controlled German radio propaganda being broadcast to Ireland in both Irish and English. Dillon seems to have been the only politician who was prepared to scrutinise the activities of the German colony who had been resident in Ireland before the outbreak of war. (That community had always eschewed the Shelbourne as too pro-British for comfort. Their last Christmas in Ireland, complete with swastika flags, Hitler portrait, ideologically correct entertainment from Aryan children and world map of German shipping lines, was celebrated in the Gresham.) Dillon, however, probably unwittingly furnished Bowen with excellent raw material for her reports. He was outraged when he discovered, years later that his private conversations with her had been reported to the British Government.

Neutral Dublin was almost as rife with intrigue and espionage as Casablanca. The German, Japanese, Italian, American and British missions were absorbed in war games. The host country, as a non-player was sometimes given rather short service. When the first American G.I.s arrived in the North in 1942, de Valera made an official complaint that the Irish government had been consulted about this imposition by neither the United States nor Britain. Roosevelt, his mind no doubt on more pressing issues, returned a brief reply by cable, saying simply: 'Really'?

In *The Shelbourne Hotel*, Bowen describes the cloak and dagger element of wartime denizens of the hotel: 'mystery men with sealed lips and locked briefcases shot through the hall and up and down in the lift.' Nobody would ever have guessed that the blameless Mrs Cameron, scribbling at a writing table or chatting to hotel residents like Rose, Dowager Marchioness of Headfort, was engaged in the same ancient profession.

In an interview given to *The Bell* in the Shelbourne in 1942 she asserted:

> As long as I can remember I've been extremely conscious of being Irish – going backwards and forwards between Ireland and England and the Continent has never robbed me of any feeling of my nationality. I must say it's a highly disturbing emotion.

Nevertheless, conforming to the established decencies of the Shelbourne, she registered her nationality on arrival as either English or British. Like many otherwise well-educated ascendancy folk she could overlook the minutiae of Irish history. In *The Shelbourne Hotel*, Charles Stuart Parnell is described as a County Meath squire and one report, sent to the Foreign Office in 1940, bespeaks a certain aloofness from popular, native culture.

Speaking of the Gaelic Revival she mentions:

> A festival – in full swing in Dublin last week – took place in the Mansion House. Plays, singing and conferences appeared to compose the programme. I say 'appeared' because all reports were printed in Irish, which I cannot read, For the same reason – I did not attend any of the sessions. As a gathering of people (largely teachers) from all over Ireland, they would have been interesting to see.

Graham Greene contended that writers are, essentially, fifth columnists. The DNA of colonialism that entwines itself through Bowen's 'Irishness' left her semi-detached from both Ireland and England. Her subconscious loyalty was reserved, fundamentally, for her own kind. In an interview with *The Bell* given in the Shelbourne she discussed the Irish novel:

> When that really Great Irish novel comes to be written, I fancy you'll find that it has been written by a Protestant who understands Catholicism and who, very probably, has made a mixed marriage.

For a fellow writer and compatriot to ignore James Joyce's seminal contribution in this context is inexplicable but members of Bowen's class and generation were conditioned to be frankly and fearlessly judgmental. Four years later, during her first postwar summer at Bowen's Court the woman who had, as a child, considered politeness to the British a form of pity, wrote to William Plomer:

> I'd much rather live my life here. I've been gradually coming unstuck from England for a long time. I have adored England since 1940 because of the stylishness Mr Churchill gave it, but I can't stick all these little middle-

> class Labour wets with their Old London School of Economics ties and their women.

The texture of the time is reproduced in Derek Mahon's poem: 'At the Shelbourne (Elizabeth Bowen, November 1940)':

Sunrise in the Irish Sea, dawn over Dublin Bay
after a stormy night, one shivering star;
and I picture the harsh waking everywhere,
the devastations of a world at war,
airfields, radio silence, a darkened convoy
strung out in moonlight on a glittering sea.
Harsh the wide windows of the hotel at daybreak
as I light up the first ciggie of the day,
stormy the lake like the one in Regent's Park,
glittering the first snow on the Wicklow hills.
Out back, a precipitous glimpse of silent walls,
courtyards, skylights of kitchen and heating plant,
seagulls in rising steam; while at the front
I stand at ease to hear a kettle sing
In an upper room of the Kildare St. wing
admiring the frosty housetops of my birthplace
miraculously immune (almost) to bomb damage.
Sun through south facing windows lights again
on the oval portrait and the polished surface
where, at an Empire writing table, I set down
my situation reports for the Dominions Office,
pen sketches of MacEntee, James Dillon and the rest,
letters to friends in Cork or Gower St.
– Virginia, Rosamond and the Horizon set –
bright novelistic stuff, a nation on the page:

'...deep, rather futile talks. It is hard afterwards
to remember the drift, though I remember words,
that smoke screen use of words! Mostly I meet
the political people; they are very religious.'
There is nothing heroic or 'patriotic' about this;
for here in this rentier heaven of racing chaps,
journalists, cipher clerks, even Abwehr types
and talkative day trippers down from Belfast,
the Mata Hari of the austerity age,

I feel like a traitor spying on my own past.
It was here the ill fate of cities happened first –
a cruiser in the Liffey, field-guns trained on the GPO,
the kicking in of doors, dances cancelled, revolvers
served with morning tea on silver salvers,
a ghostly shipboard existence down below,
people asleep in corridors as now
in the London Underground, mysterious Kor,
a change of uniforms in the cocktail bar
though the bronze slave girls still stand where they were,
Nubian in aspect, in manner art-nouveau.
I must get the Austin out of the garage,
drive down this week-end to Bowen's Court
if I can find petrol, and back for the Sunday mail-boat –
though this is home really, a place of warmth and light,
a house of artifice neither here nor there
between the patrician past and the egalitarian future,
tempting one always to prolong one's visit:
in war, peace, rain or fog you couldn't miss it
however late the hour, however dark the night.

One of the 'mystery men' whom Bowen probably saw shooting in and out of the lobby and up and down in the lift was Martin S. Quigley, a secret agent sent here by the Office of Strategic Services of the U.S. Joint Chiefs of Staff. His cover was commercial work on behalf of the American film industry and, by the end of his sojourn, this, rather than his espionage activities, had made him unwelcome to the establishment. Draconian censorship and the militant pursuit of neutrality kept the Irish public completely insulated from the rest of the world. Newsreels had any material pertinent to the War excised and replaced by footage of animals in Dublin Zoo and the Emergency Powers Orders sanctioned such radical cuts that film plots became unintelligible.

Quigley's cover involved lobbying for freedom of information and greater access to American entertainment. By the end of his stay he reports:

> I would not have been very surprised had I been asked to leave Eire, and I feel pretty sure any request for an extension of my stay beyond November 15 would not have been well received. This does not concern my cover which, I believe, is firmly established in all quarters … but my cover activity became annoying or objectionable to the Irish authorities.

In fact Quigley's campaign for liberalisation resulted in the censorship authorities tightening their regulations even more, effectively barring Quigley from visiting the censor's office.

Three men had been selected by the OSS for the Irish mission. The first, Erwin Ross Marlin, was sent to Dublin but his cover was blown almost immediately when the Irish censor opened OSS material which had been posted to him in the ordinary mail. The second, Roland Blenner-Hasset, stationed in Tralee, was also discovered but allowed to continue operating, probably in the hope that his reports might counterbalance the distorted intelligence emanating from David Gray, the U.S. minister here. Gray had such poor personal relations with de Valera that he was effectively cut off from useful Irish government contacts. His WASP sympathies lay with the landed gentry, Anglo-Irish commercial interests and the Protestant community generally. His wife, Maude, was the aunt of Eleanor Roosevelt, which gave Gray privileged access to the President and lent credence to reports that might otherwise have been met with scepticism since one of Gray's more bizarre sources was the ghost of A.J. Balfour, the deceased British prime minister.

The American agents seem to have been unsympathetic not only to Gray but to each other. In fact, when Washington decided to post agents to Ireland one of the first volunteers to propose himself was Errol Flynn, whose father had been a Professor at Queen's University, Belfast. Quigley's arrival injected a note of sanity into an eccentric situation. The Shelbourne became his base for the duration of his stay. His first report, was dated from the hotel on 29 May 1943:

> Walter McNally, RKO Radio pictures distributor and operator of several theatres and cafés, met me at the boat on Tuesday evening. He had reserved a room for me at

> the Shelbourne. That was fortunate, for it is extremely difficult to get a hotel room in this city. There are many visitors.

He was assigned a single bedroom with bathroom, overlooking Stephen's Green. Initially, he had intended to move on to a smaller hotel but he never did.

> That was my room wherever I was in Dublin, I would give it up during my trips to provincial cities and towns ... but on returning to the Shelbourne I was always assigned to the same room. The price uniformly was one pound per night. I always had breakfast in the Shelbourne dining room and often had lunch there, usually with a guest from the entertainment or media world.

The Shelbourne diet which seemed so plentiful to fugitives from British rationing was less lavish for an American. In a few months Quigley lost twenty pounds in weight and was prescribed a daily pint of Guinness by his doctor. Shelbourne menus at that time notified guests that it was illegal to serve butter at luncheons or dinners or bread at luncheons, dinners or suppers.

Quigley's reports, which were de-classified in 1997, give a bemused but thorough account of the censorship culture here. Coming from a nation as diverse as the United States the divisions of Irish society intrigued him:

> The Anglo-Irishman in Dublin, even after generations, evidently does not understand the native Irish at all ... It is somewhat strange because most of the native Irish have in their blood much the same strain as the English but it seems that many or most of the Anglo-Irish still consider themselves foreigners here.

Residence in the Shelbourne undoubtedly informed his views of the Ascendancy.

In 1984 Martin Quigley and his wife spent a holiday in Ireland and stayed in the Shelbourne. Coming downstairs one day he bumped into Dan Bryan on the mezzanine. They started chatting about old times.

Quigley had always surmised that Bryan had some suspicions about his wartime activities in Ireland and he confessed that his film business had been a cover for intelligence work. Dan Bryan was astounded and assured Quigley that, of all the foreign nationals here, he had been the only one above suspicion.

Although the Shelbourne was first and foremost a Protestant enclave it entertained a degree of pluralism when the circumstances were appropriate. The racing and hunting fraternity, particularly, had always managed to straddle all divides. For true devotees, the cult of the horse transcends any other crude accidents of religion or race. Some of the country's more distinguished and celebrated Catholics were valued patrons too. The tenor, John McCormack, who was created a Papal Count in 1928 was one of these. He died of throat cancer in September 1945, at the age of 61 in his home, Glena, in Blackrock. Before moving in there he was a resident in the Shelbourne for eighteen months. His health, at that time, was not good and his wife believed that the rigours of his British wartime tours were responsible for his decline. The Count had retired prior to the outbreak of war and his return to the concert circuit was his way of repaying the support and opportunities which he had enjoyed in Britain.

McCormack was one of Ireland's most illustrious exports. He was raised respectably but frugally in Athlone and professional success and romance came early and with apparent ease. He was still in his teens when he first met his wife, Lily Foley, another gifted singer. They were both awarded gold medals at the Feis Ceóil in 1903, John winning the tenor's section and Lily the Irish solo soprano. Success at the Feis, Ireland's national amateur music competition, launched many distinguished musical careers.

Luigi Denza, the adjudicator at the following year's Feis, may have done an oblique service to literature too when he withheld the gold medal from a promising but optically challenged performer who declined to attempt a sight reading exercise. Because of this refusal James Joyce was only awarded a bronze medal which, according to Oliver St John Gogarty, he tossed into the Liffey as it could not be pawned. Later that year, Joyce and McCormack shared the concert platform in the Antient Concert Rooms and their friendship endured. Joyce had inherited his love of music from his own father, John Stanislaus Joyce. Years afterwards, in Paris, he wrote to McCormack after a concert:

> How delighted we were by your singing, especially the aria from *Don Giovanni.* I have lived in Italy practically ever since we last met but no Italian lyrical tenor that I know (Bonci possibly excepting) could do such a feat of breathing and phrasing – to say nothing of the beauty of tone.

John and Lily McCormack's marriage took place in 1906 and remained a model of mutual devotion to the end. That same year was an eventful one for the tenor. He obtained some contracts to record songs for the newly invented gramophone and used the proceeds to take himself and his wife to Italy, where he trained with the great Sabatini. He made his Italian opera debut at Savona, that same year. In a concession to Italian operatic chauvinism, he borrowed Lily's surname and styled himself Giovanni Foli for his first appearances in that country but the name McCormack was to become famous in three continents very quickly.

The following year McCormack became the youngest ever tenor, at the age of twenty-three, to sing in a major role in Covent Garden when he sang the role of Turiddu in *Cavalliere Rusticana.* He had been fortunate in gaining an entrée to the London musical world through the patronage of John Murray Scott. In 1909, McCormack was signed by Oscar Hammerstein for a season in New York and returned to sing with Dame Nellie Melba in London and Sydney.

He was a genial man, free of the temperament that is often associated with performing stars and was generous, at times almost to a fault. Jewels, racehorses, paintings and property were irresistible to him but many of his extravagances were purely magnanimous. Lily's brother and sister-in-law were lost at sea when the mail boat *Leinster* was torpedoed in Dublin Bay. Their ten children were orphaned by the tragedy. McCormack, although already committed to supporting his own parents, unhesitatingly undertook the expenses of their upbringing and education and adopted the youngest child.

John Count McCormack in informal mode.

He was also unstinting in his praise for fellow artists, a characteristic that was shared by his close friend, Caruso. Once, when they met by chance McCormack exclaimed: 'How is the world's greatest tenor today?' and elicited the gracious response: 'That, my friend, you must tell me.' Fritz Kreisler, who played the obligato accompaniment to McCormack's best-selling record *Panis Angelicus* was another close friend.

Although his grandson, the present John Count McCormack, was not born until two years after his grandfather's death his grandmother survived her husband by twenty-six years, keeping his memory alive for her grandchildren. John junior and his sisters, Tish and Carol Ann all know the family anecdotes well. Their grandfather's champagne drinking was taken almost as seriously as his music. Prior to concerts the Count would avoid speaking to anybody. If he had to communicate at all he would whisper in order to conserve his voice. Just as religiously, he concluded the evening's entertainment with a bottle of Pol Roger. No other brand would suffice. McCormack, a cheerful *bon vivant*, found champagne appropriate for many occasions. In the course of his last long stay in the Shelbourne, the cellar ran dry of the favoured champagne. No doubt the exigencies of wartime rather than the Count's consumption was responsible for this depletion but the management was embarrassed by their inability to supply the requirements of such an esteemed guest. The Shelbourne's *sommeliers* were despatched to comb the city for fresh supplies but had no success. None of the city's smarter establishments could oblige. There was a national drought of Pol Roger. Hope had almost been abandoned when, at last they located a stock in a most unexpected place. The Dawson Lounge, around the corner from the Shelbourne in Dawson Street, is a tiny basement bar, which has maintained its licence on the same premises since 1850. Apparently their wartime patrons had been content with more modest libations.

Today's John McCormack owns the QV2 restaurant on Dublin's St Andrew Street, a popular haunt of film and theatre people. In spite of the demands of his business, the present Count is also a singer and has brought a contemporary idiom to the family tradition as a vocalist with his popular rock and roll band, Dave and the Be-bops. At one of their recent gigs, they played in the Shelbourne's Great Room at the Glenstal Abbey school leavers' dance. Inevitably there was one voice of dissent among the accolades of enthusiasm. One ultra-conservative parent remarked cholerically that the racket must be making the grandfather turn in his grave. It is not likely. Like his grandson the first Count McCormack had a finely tuned instinct for the nuances of popular taste.

The intelligence operatives had faded away with the return of peace but the musk of intrigue still lingered. The Shelbourne entertained its share of lovers, among them Graham Greene and Catherine Walston. Their turbulent affair began in 1947 and lasted for at least thirteen years. Much of it was played out in Ireland, either at the cottage which Catherine Walston owned on Achill Island or in Dublin.

Catherine Walston, an American beauty, married to one of the richest men in England and the mother of six children was described by Evelyn Waugh as 'unaffected to the verge of insanity'. Ian Fleming's wife, Ann, giving an account of her eccentric behaviour concluded: 'she's a very maddening woman.' A relationship with a man as driven and complex as Greene was doomed to be stormy. Catherine initiated the first contact between them when she wrote to Greene asking him to stand as her godfather at her reception into the Catholic church. Their affair was, therefore, not only illicit but sacrilegious. The spiritual relationship running parallel to the sexual one created the sort of dark dichotomy which Greene adored.

They shared a taste for mysticism, attending mass together and travelling to Italy to visit Padre Pio and various shrines and 'breathing' statues. In fact, Catherine's conversion to Catholicism had an unconventional subtext. She found religion a powerful erotic stimulant, and celibate Catholic priests excited her more than Anglican ones. One of the great attractions of Dublin was that it was awash with Catholic priests, particularly Father Donal O'Sullivan who later became head of the Irish Arts Council. Her long affair with Greene did not inhibit her obsession with men of the cloth.

In 1948 Greene began to write *The End Of The Affair*, a fictionalised account of the triangular relationship between himself, Catherine, and her husband, Harry. Friends were shocked by how closely the novel mimicked the real life names, events and conversations of the relationship. Greene's routine was to write five hundred words a day regardless of where he was or what was happening in his private life. During the two years while he was working on *The End Of The Affair* many of his daily writing stints took place in the Shelbourne. The Walstons had a flat in Dublin for a time but many of Greene's letters to Catherine were addressed to her at the Shelbourne. At other times they stayed or dined there together. Writing to Catherine in New York from Saigon on 4 February 1952, Greene tells her that a New York paper, arrived that morning, contains, 'an article on the Shelbourne Hotel and daren't I read it. I so loved Ireland and now we never go ...'

CHAPTER SIX

PEACETIME PROGRESS

Do you know what my ambition is when I get money? To ... strut in through the front door ... and into the Shelbourne Rooms. They say it's the most beautiful bar in the world.

Colonel Jury's son, Captain Peter Jury, had been born in India in 1919 when his father was serving in the army. His mother had died when he was young and he had been brought up subsequently by her sister, Dorothy, who later married the Colonel. After completing his secondary education at Rugby he joined his father's old regiment the 13th /18th Hussars. During World War II he was stationed in North Africa. After 17 years at the helm, Colonel Edward Jury had decided to retire from active involvement in the day to day business of the Shelbourne. In fact, like many other patriarchs of family businesses he found it impossible to stay away from the place subsequently, but officially Peter Jury was placed in charge.

Stephen Fairburn Cotton had died and the chairmanship of the private company had passed to Colonel Jury's father, Charles Cotton Jury.

The Colonel was a bewhiskered, barking, Kipling character whose militaristic style of management had aroused trepidation at all staff levels. The Captain, in spite of having been fathered by such an old war horse, was gentle, retiring and rather shy. Although he had no previous direct experience of the hotel business he had been born into the Cotton Jury family so one suspects there was innate hoteliership in his genes. He soon demonstrated a shrewd grasp of contemporary market trends. Although he had inherited a venerable institution it had changed too little during the past few decades. Survival and success in the post-war world would, he realised, demand a sharper competitive edge.

In 1946, before he officially took over the management he had been preparing for his new role. He had enquired from William White of Atkins Chirnside, Accountants, in Cork about his future remuneration as a director of the company. This, he learned, was not to exceed £250 per annum in addition to travelling and hotel expenses. Once installed, he set about expanding and improving the business.

In 1949 number 33 St Stephen's Green was acquired for £5,000. Annual ground rent was £96/6/10 and the Poor Law Valuation was £127. The extra space was badly needed. Since the war ended the hotel had been filled to capacity and had been turning away custom. An application to extend the licence to cover number 31 listed the numbers of visitors who had been refused accommodation during the preceding year.

During the peak season these figures were running at over five hundred a month. Business had increased threefold since 1940 and stamp records over those years showed a refusal rate running, at periods, up to forty or fifty per day. The four-storey over-basement premises would, it was projected, house another twenty-five guests. It would also inspire Peter Jury with the germ of another project, which would be a further ten years in coming to fruition but would result in the opening of the Shelbourne Ballroom.

In the spring of 1950 he initiated a massive programme of reconstruction and refurbishment. An extension was added to number 33 and bathrooms multiplied like pond amoebae. It was a far cry from the days when McCurdy's new building had opened with just fifteen en suite bathrooms.

He also started grooming and recruiting new management executives. Bernard Molloy, who had been manager since 1937, was joined by some new assistants. One of them was Padraic McCarville Browne who started his thirty-five year career in the Shelbourne in 1948. Peter Jury also hired a young secretary, Mary Holohan, who would spend the next twelve years in the hotel, moving from secretarial work to an assistantship in the rapidly developing functions area.

During those years, life in the hotel reflected the emergence of a new social order in the surrounding city. The declaration of the Irish Republic in 1949 marked a significant step in Ireland's transformation to a European state.

People who worked there at the time remember the fifties as a time when the 'mere Irish' began to use the hotel and mingle with the old establishment. Those who did, however, were still a privileged minority. Most Dubliners had to make do with more accessible venues, like the indigent American students of J.P. Donleavy's *The Gingerman.*

> In the eight o'clock sound and smell of Jury's lounge they sat with stretched legs and toes twitching in their shoes, thawing damp bones in the centrally heated air. Priests scattered through the room, red faced watery eyed and smouldering.

O'Keefe wistfully imparts his fantasies to Dangerfield:

> Do you know what my ambition is when I get money? To move into the Shelbourne Hotel. Strut in through the front door and tell the porter would you garage my Daimler for me please – and into the Shelbourne Rooms. They say it's the most beautiful bar in the world.

The Shelbourne Rooms, formerly the gracious ground-floor apartments of Lord de Montault's town house certainly constituted the most elegant cocktail bar in the city. They could be accessed either by a curving staircase from the writing room, later to become the Horseshoe Bar, or from St Stephen's Green. The guest list for the official opening on 23 November 1944 was drawn from the cream of the city's social register, many of them permanent residents in the hotel. Rose, Marchioness of

Headfort, who lived in room 77, attended with her companion Miss Pearson.

The Marchioness had a colourful history. She had become the toast of the town when she came from England, as a Gaiety Girl, to perform in the Gaiety Theatre. The arrival of these itinerant Edwardian beauties had done much to enliven the ambience of the Shelbourne at the turn of the century. They were talented, lively, charming and accessible. They must have been anathema to the matchmaking mothers of the day.

Many of them married into the peerage or gentry but few as brilliantly as Rosie Boote who became, as Lady Headfort, chatelaine of one of the country's most magnificent estates near Kells, County Meath. It must have caused society's Protestant matrons further chagrin that Rosie, a devout Catholic, converted the Headfort dynasty to Rome. Her beauty continued to dazzle admirers for many years, among them Augustus John, who sketched her portrait on the wall of a summer house in the Headfort park.

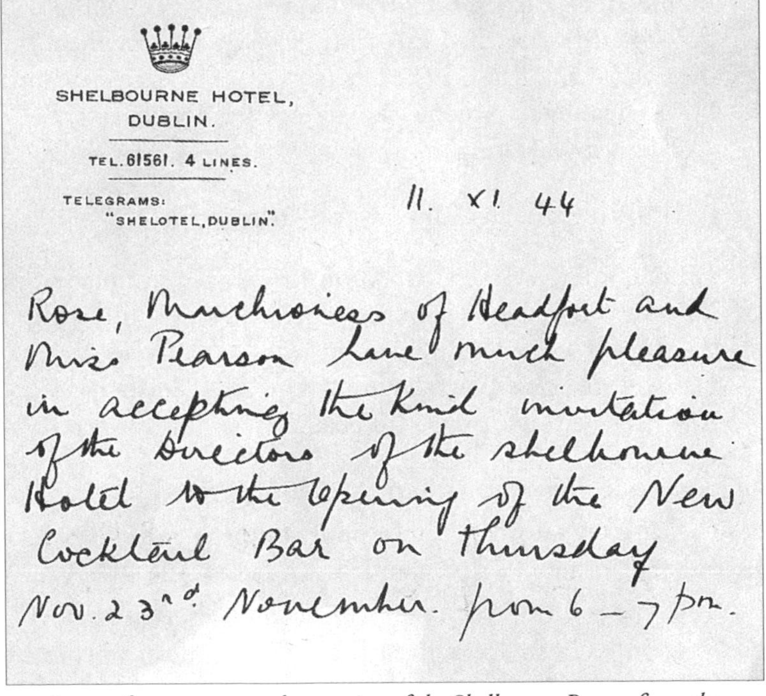

SHELBOURNE HOTEL,
DUBLIN.

TEL. 61561. 4 LINES.

TELEGRAMS:
"SHELOTEL, DUBLIN."

11. XI. 44

Rose, Marchioness of Headfort and Miss Pearson have much pleasure in accepting the kind invitation of the Directors of the Shelbourne Hotel to the Opening of the New Cocktail Bar on Thursday Nov. 23rd November. from 6 – 7 pm.

Letter of acceptance to the opening of the Shelbourne Rooms from the Marchioness of Headfort.

Elizabeth Bowen, in a letter to Charles Ritchie, describes meeting her in the Shelbourne:

> … a most heavenly woman, the Dowager Lady Headford, who used to be Rosie Boot [sic], the most cracking Edwardian beauty. She still wears her hair à la 1910 and wore the most nostalgically beautiful black hat trimmed with a wreath of flaming white marguerites. You know what really terrific personalities on the Proust scale those stars of the Gaiety and Dolly's who married into the peerage were. They must have had something much subtler and less drearily biological than what is now called sex appeal.

Interior of the Shelbourne Rooms cocktail bar.

After that first meeting the two spent many hours gossiping together in the Shelbourne Rooms. The 1944 opening was reported in *The Irish Times*:

> A cocktail bar, to blend with the pastel colouring and period furniture of two exquisite Georgian rooms, is the newest addition to the Shelbourne Hotel Dublin.
>
> The rooms which adjoin are decorated in pale blue and white. The original colours of the Adam medallions on the walls have been reproduced with unusual taste and restraint. Along the walls are long couches with graceful golden legs. There are chairs and tables similarly

> graceful in the delicate Georgian style with big bowls of fresh flowers here and there.
>
> One of the main problems was to devise a bar with its necessary equipment that would not clash with Georgian architecture. In this, the architects Messrs O'Connor and Aylward have succeeded admirably. Here the indirect pale blue lighting is most effective.
>
> The Shelbourne Rooms, as they have been named, were formally opened on Thursday evening when guests were received by the Managing Director of the hotel, Colonel E.C. Jury and Mrs. Jury. The Manager Mr. Bernard C. Molloy was also present to supervise the opening.
>
> The contractors were Messrs J.F. Keatinge and Sons Ltd.

Although the new facility was in keeping with the dignified character of the hotel, its ambience made the place seem less frostily exclusive. With the single boisterous exception of the Dublin Horse Show week, the Shelbourne year had always revolved in a dignified hush. This was especially true of the dining room, an almost moribund sanctum patronised exclusively by residents. Although the fare was more palatable than the 'cold mutton in a draught' of traditional Big House cuisine the atmosphere was not festive. Noisy, lively private parties were confined to other rooms. The Shelbourne's restrained atmosphere had never encouraged non-residents to drop in casually but the fifties saw the start of a gradual infiltration.

The poet, John Montague, recalls his brother inviting him to lunch there in the early fifties. It was a rare treat but gaining admission presented some difficulties. The head waiter, obviously reluctant to admit the Montague brothers without a struggle, fixed upon the point that the poet was not wearing a tie. His brother, undeterred, told John to stay put while he went round to Tyson's in Grafton Street to buy one, after which they sat down and lunched in style. For John Montague, it was the start of a lifelong relationship with the place which is still his first pit stop whenever he arrives in town.

By the mid-fifties complex plans were afoot to develop the functions business. Padraic Browne spent two years at the Dorchester in London, acquiring the skills necessary for streamlining this part of the Shelbourne's operations. For a while he was joined in London by the banqueting head waiter Claude Spillane. Claude, who presided over the banqueting services from 1952 to 1980 had been christened Tadgh but had changed his name for reasons of professional aesthetics. The chef, Eugene Lucien Martin, came from London's Savoy Grill and Mary Holohan also worked for a spell at the Savoy to broaden her experience. The banqueting team who reassembled at the Shelbourne in 1956 were second to none. The construction of a new ballroom was under way behind numbers 32 and 33 St Stephen's Green.

This brainchild, conceived by Peter Jury when he arrived at the Shelbourne in 1947, had taken nearly ten years to come to fruition. The official opening took place on 2 October 1956. From then on the emerging bourgeoisie of the city would flock to the new ballroom to quick-step, waltz, foxtrot, tango, even rock and roll to the music of Earl Gill's Band.

Earl Gill was only twenty-three when he became the resident Shelbourne band leader. He had already had a long career in the world of professional entertainment, playing in theatres from the age of twelve and becoming lead trumpeter with the Neil Kearns orchestra at the Gresham when he was seventeen. In 1953, he formed his own band. The repertoire of many dance bands had barely changed since the war. Gill's group was young and versatile and added rock and jazz numbers to the standard dance band programmes.

The panel who auditioned candidates for the job in the ballroom consisted of Peter Jury, Barney Molloy and a maintenance man who had been included on the panel because of his proficiency on the accordion. As soon as the decision had been made, Gill set about augmenting and re-organising his ensemble, with the total co-operation of Peter Jury who took a keen interest in music. From then on, Gill's band were always the first in the city to play the latest music from new Broadway shows. Peter Jury would procure all the latest sheet music on his trips to America and bring it back to the Shelbourne long before it had been published on this side of the Atlantic.

Earl Gill (second from left) and his band with Count Basie.

Gill's band, like the ballroom itself, was the last word in sophistication. They remained the resident band until 1965, when the success of their 'Hoedowners' television series sent them off on permanent tour for a period of ten years, after which they returned to the Shelbourne in the mid-seventies.

The innovative structure of the new ballroom, incorporating a pyramid roof, suspended ceiling and gallery, was designed by Michael Scott, Ireland's foremost architect at that time. Since implementing Captain Jury's refurbishment of the hotel in 1950, he had built an international reputation. His pioneering work in hospital design, his own house in Sandycove, the Irish Pavilion at the New York World Fair and Busaras, the city bus station brought Irish architecture into the post-Corbusier era.

Michael Scott's wife, Patricia, a noted beauty who had featured in advertisements for Pond's Face Cream, ran the Lilac Room which housed the hotel beauty parlour. The interior of the Lilac Room and much of the ballroom interior was decorated by Patrick Scott, best known now as a painter and abstract tapestry designer. Although he had presented his first one man show in 1944 he was then still practising as an architect, and did not become a full-time artist until 1960.

The ballroom was a showcase for many rising talents. At a time when Dublin's Georgian vistas were being devoured by modernism of doubtful quality, Scott's imaginative, state-of-the-art ballroom did nothing to impinge on the existing 1770 façade of numbers 32 and 33 St Stephen's Green. Apart from widening a doorway the exteriors were left intact. The entrance foyer, too, retained much of the original architectural character. The transition into a contemporary ballroom was dramatic. The square dance floor was surrounded on all sides by a sitting out area under a cantilevered, reinforced balcony. The central ceiling was vaulted in the form of an octagonal pyramid, giving the impression of a huge circus tent, and the balconies were tiered to three distinct levels affording a view of the band from every point. The walls were exotically papered in jet black with a white print of Redouté roses. Dancers could rejoice in the latest Floating Floor, made of seasoned maple and the carpets, designed by Louis le Brocquy, were inspired by the neolithic symbols of Newgrange. The lighting system could provide twenty-three different hues and tints and the air conditioning was so efficient that no windows were necessary. The sound systems were state of the art. Structurally, technically and socially it was the city's most sophisticated venue.

Chefs at the Ballroom opening night supper. Maurice O' Looney is on the far right. Alan Gleeson is third from right.

Yet there were some last minute problems. There was an objection to a permanent canopy which had been erected at the ballroom entrance. This projection from the building contravened a law of 1862. The Lord Mayor, Robert Briscoe, officiating at the opening ceremony, said that he wished the regulations of Dublin Corporation could be as progressive as the ideas of citizens who could conceive and build such a wonderful amenity. He had instructed Michael Scott to go ahead with the job in spite of the law. As a constant visitor of thirty years standing in the hotel he had, he said, at all times received the greatest consideration and courtesy.

The first night's gala ball in aid of the Central Remedial Clinic was the grandest of occasions. Earl Gill's band opened, shortly after ten o'clock, with 'Let's Do It' and Lady Valerie Goulding, the patron of the clinic, led off the dance partnered by Mr William Murphy. As a fundraiser it was a huge success. The room was full to capacity with four hundred guests who had paid three guineas each for their tickets. The Shelbourne took only twelve shillings and sixpence per head to subsidise the night's entertainment.

Noel Coward came in from the world première of his play, *Nude With A Violin*, at the Olympia and spoke. He had been asked to sing but, as he explained in a letter to Peter Jury:

> I am dreadfully sorry to disappoint you and Lady Goulding but I am coming to Dublin specifically to work on my new play and shall have only ten days in which to do all that has to be done. Secondly I shall have no accompanist available – and even if it were possible to procure one, it would mean a great deal of rehearsing. However, if it would be of any help to the Shelbourne, Lady Goulding and the charity, I will appear at the Ball and do anything to help which would not involve preliminary rehearsals.
>
> I am so looking forward to coming to Dublin again and staying at the Shelbourne.

The list of guests which was published in the *Tatler and Bystander* was a catalogue of the titled, the horsey and the chic who had always frequented the hotel but, as time went by the ballroom would host a more eclectic cross-section of Irish life than the Shelbourne had seen before. The détente generated its own teething problems. Competition was fierce to secure a booking for one of the opening days of the new facility. One of the prestigious début evenings was secured by Conradh na Gaelige. At the last moment, to the consternation of the management, they cancelled.

The organisation had received an unexpected acceptance from an Uachtaráin, Seán T. O'Kelly to preside over their dinner as guest of honour. Certain members of the organisation decided that it would be impolitic to entertain the President of the eight-year-old republic in such an 'English' stronghold as the Shelbourne.

It was unthinkable that the new ballroom should have a cancellation in its first week of business, especially one with such an overtly political agenda. A go-between was needed to solve the problem and Seamus O'Kelly of *The Irish Times* was co-opted. He was often in the hotel monitoring the social whirl for his 'Quidnunc' column. Apart from being well acquainted with the Shelbourne management he was able to approach the other parties and was also a personal friend of the President, so he was despatched to Phoenix Park in an attempt to limit the damage.

The President's response was gallant and obliging. He would, he assured Kelly, be more than happy to spend an evening in the Shelbourne provided that a full bottle of whiskey was provided at his table. The dinner went off well, was highly publicised and did much to ensure the credibility of the Shelbourne's new banqueting facility.

In many ways, Ireland in the fifties was still mired in a time warp where the entire community had to negotiate a permanent minefield of faith and morals. Censorship was still thriving with all sorts of innocuous fare figuring on the banned list. Mixed bathing could provoke convulsions of prudery and some cinemas even segregated the sexes, making exceptions only for post-mature married couples. Sectarianism simmered beneath the surface, rising to the boil occasionally in such disturbing episodes as the Fethard-on-Sea Boycott in 1957 in which an entire Wexford village became Balkanised when a child attended the Protestant rather than the Catholic school. At that time the *Ne Temere* decree imposing Catholic education on all children of mixed marriages was threatening the dwindling Protestant community with extinction. The Catholic majority in Fethard, spurred on by meddlesome members of the clergy, made a public issue of a private decision and mounted a boycott, bringing financial ruin to some Protestants and driving others out of the area. The Protestant community of the twenty-six counties was then no more than two or three per cent of the population. It is easy to understand why this

The dining room in the 1950s

isolated minority clung to institutions like the Shelbourne which offered a secure haven in which to meet co-religionists and prospective spouses.

The business community had to contend with other problems. Practices which would have been intolerable in any other European state went unchecked. In 1951 the banks went on strike. The economy was left to function as best it could on cheques scribbled on scraps of paper and back of envelopes, often endorsed and circulated through several transactions. The temptations for anyone of less than perfect probity are obvious. As a virtual economy it worked surprisingly well up to the point when the banks re-opened. In spite of the devastating effect which this had on private individuals and businesses alike, it was a situation which would proceed unchecked until the late seventies.

Yet this reactionary society was unwittingly poised on the brink of a economic quantum leap. The pragmatism of Lemass was about to supersede the frugal piety of de Valera. Free trade would eclipse self sufficiency. There was cautious optimism in the air. The country just might be able to make a transition from agrarianism to technology without the intervening blight of an industrial revolution. Lemass was the visionary who set these wheels of change revolving. In those days he treated the Shelbourne like a private club, hosting a Friday night poker game for close friends in a private room on the first floor. The sessions began punctually at 5.30 p.m. every Saturday evening and went on until about 4.00 a.m. on Sunday morning. The core players were Mr Crowley, who was permanently resident in room 205, Mr Woods and Mr Frank McGrath. Other players were invited to augment the group over the years and strict control was exercised over staff entering the room where the game was in session. One waiter was selected to be the sole attendant at the weekly party. Initially, this role was entrusted to John Crowley. He was succeeded, when he left, by Dickie Cockburn and subsequently by John Melia. When Lemass became Taoiseach in 1959 the first floor poker school went into abeyance.

A different breed of businessman had arrived and the Shelbourne swung easily on its hinges to accommodate him. In 1956 a Frenchman, Raymond Girault, moved into the hotel with his wife and three children. His business was to establish IBM in Ireland. He was representing the first major international company to exploit the possibilities of Ireland as a market base. Interviews were conducted on the mezzanine landing, where the fountain had once tinkled in John McCurdy's Winter Garden. The sophisticated recruitment and assessment techniques of the multinational corporation were totally foreign to Irish executives. Derek Overend, IBM's first Irish employee can still recall his bewilderment when an attractive female interviewer invited him to step into a nearby bedroom for an aptitude test.

IBM had been founded in the States in 1928 by the Watsons, a Quaker family with rigid business ethics. In Ireland, as everywhere else, their executive conduct was governed by inflexible rules. No client could ever be entertained until after a contract was signed and no gifts or hospitality could ever be received by sales staff. In the *laisser faire* environment of Dublin business this no-fun ethic gave rise to misunderstandings. IBM executives often had to resort to entertaining disgruntled clients in discreet privacy at considerable personal expense.

Having started with only a handful of staff, IBM grew rapidly, initiating the first dawn of Ireland's information age. As the company grew it retained its loyalty to the Shelbourne, holding family dinners, children's parties and corporate celebrations there. The most popular fixtures in the company calendar are still the pre-Rugby International luncheons held in the Constitution Room.

CHAPTER SEVEN

THE DEAR TOLERANT SHELBOURNE

If Dublin had a back door it was the front door to the Shelbourne.

Sally Abrahams was a student in T.C.D. when she met Peter Jury. They were married in 1953 in St Paul's, Knightsbridge. At the wedding reception, hosted by Sally's parents, Major General and Mrs Abrahams, an old Shelbourne skeleton rattled out of the closet. The bridegroom had taken Paddy Kelly, the Shelbourne's most senior porter, to London with him to act as valet for the period of the wedding trip. Kelly, who was then in his seventies, could be relied upon to do a good job under the scrutiny of the new, English in-laws. The bride's family were liberal hosts and Paddy Kelly was not excluded from their hospitality. In a moment of alcohol induced confidence, he revealed a secret which he had kept for thirty-seven years. Kelly, who had apparently been blamelessly employed in the hotel for the duration of the Easter Rising, had been a secret intelligence operative. Unknown to both colleagues and management he had made stealthy access to the roof at frequent intervals to signal with flags to the rebels in St Stephen's Green.

not operating alone. Later information suggested that also supplying Countess Markiewicz' battalion with e Shelbourne roof. The various people involved in nating information from the hotel must have been er, as the roof, although extensive, could hardly have been mmodating competing teams of spies. It was ironic that this long-buried revolutionary secret was finally unlocked by a surfeit of British hospitality.

Sally Jury.

The newly wed Jurys settled in Killiney and launched into a hectic social whirl. International celebrities were arriving in the Shelbourne in ever increasing numbers and they met them all. Sally Jury became one of the city's leading hostesses. On a typical, quiet evening in 1954 the Captain and his bride hosted an intimate supper party to mark the close of a run of *Blithe Spirit* in the Gaiety. The author, Noel Coward and the star, Kay Kendall, were present. The latter, *Irish Tatler and Sketch* reported:

> was even more bewitching in real life than she appears on the stage, she wore a slinky black lace dress which looked lovely with her fair skin and specially dyed-for-the-part silvery hair. Mrs Jury, looked delightfully pretty and très très chic in a midnight blue and black printed brocade.

Every party given in the hotel included certain invisible presences who knew everyone in the room but whose names never figured in the social columns. They were the members of staff, models of courteous attention while on duty and irreverently acute later, in the privacy of their own quarters. Gabriel Walsh, who started work as a commis waiter in 1954 describes the world behind the green baize door in his forthcoming autobiography *Maggie's Breakfast.*

His entry into the Shelbourne was the result of a momentary impulse but his exit from it was completely unpredictable. He was the fifth of eleven children in an impoverished Inchicore family. Life had never offered him any more than the barest subsistence until the day in his teens when he walked past the Shelbourne and detected the aroma of roasting chickens wafting through a ventilator grille. Although he had never tasted chicken in his life he recognised the smell of Dives' table:

> The Shelbourne was Dublin's best address. Old English and crusty. It had history and culture attached to it. If Dublin had a back door it was the front door to the Shelbourne – It was a different world.

The decision which he made changed his life more radically than he ever could have dreamed. He approached a hall porter who had just ushered an incoming guest out of a taxi and asked how he could get a job there. The porter gave Gabriel a drumhead vetting on the pavement and directed him to the assistant manager who was on duty. This happened to be Padraic Browne. Gabriel still remembers his decency. Waiters, unlike porters or pages, had to buy their own uniforms and Gabriel had neither the clothes nor the money to start work. Browne hired him as a commis waiter and took him down to the waiters' dressing-room where he borrowed the basic necessities from other staff.

After the exigencies of life in Inchicore the Shelbourne was another planet for Gabriel. He started on the early shift, serving breakfasts and twice a week he helped in the dining room. He came into contact with people whom he had never dreamed of meeting. On only his second day on duty in the dining room, the party of Indian dignitaries to whom he proferred the dessert trolley included Indira Gandhi, then the daughter of the Prime Minister.

In the weeks that followed he waited on such luminaries as Robert Briscoe, Dublin's future Lord Mayor and the film director John Huston. By the time he served tea to Montgomery Clift he had become sufficiently blasé to ask Clift whether he really played the trumpet in his film, *From Here to Eternity.*

He heard classical music for the first time in his life when he delivered a breakfast tray to room 210 and heard the sound of a guitar. A floor maid, her arms full of clean linen, told him that the guests next door had complained that the noise had kept them awake all night. The occupant of 210 was sitting in bed in his nightshirt, oblivious to anything other than his own plucking fingers. As Gabriel left the room he stopped playing and said, glowing with satisfaction:

> I've been trying all night to do that – It's there. It's between the chords. The quivering string is frightened. It must be made secure – Love it and it will speak its sound.

Gabriel retreated, mystified, to the service pantry where the other lad on duty was drinking a cup of tea and reading the newspaper which featured a familiar face: 'I just took him his breakfast,' Gabriel exclaimed. 'What's his name?' They read, in unison, 'Andre Segovia.'

His second musical encounter would change his life completely. As he settled into his new job he realised that his fellow staff members, who were normally resilient to the fussiness and eccentricity of guests, were, to a man, terrified of one regular incumbent and dreaded her return: As Walsh further recalls:

> When Nuala Finnegan and Mary Turlow, the fifth floor housemaids spoke about her their voices trembled:
>
> > 'Nothing is ever right. Your hands and fingernails are dirty and your slip needs starch – There's grease on your apron and soup on your shoes. The bed sheets are not properly ironed – An' she's from Mayo herself I'm told. Just a country girl from Castlebar, Mayo. I don't suppose she thinks much about that part of herself. The way she dresses up would frighten a ghost – She finds fault with everything.'

The ogress was the opera singer, Margaret Burke Sheridan. The trajectory of her career had soared from a bereaved Mayo childhood to the premier league of Italian opera. When the orphaned child was sent to the Dominican Convent in Eccles Street the potential of her voice was recognised by Sister Clements, the brilliant and perceptive amanuensis of many musical talents. Even with such a good start the road from pupil to prima donna was not easy. Her debut in Rome attracted six encores and attracted the admiration of Toscanini, who gave her three days to learn the part of Mimi in *La Bohème.* That was the beginning of a series of brilliant successes in Puccini operas. Puccini himself always said that she had made the title role of *Madame Butterfly* her own.

She was fortunate in her patronage, not least that of Marconi. His own mother, the former Annie Jameson, grand-daughter of the whiskey distiller John Jameson, had left Ireland for Bologna in the early 1860s to sing in the opera. After arriving there she met and married Giuseppe Marconi and became the mother of Guglielmo Marconi in 1874. He would have had a special understanding of the courage required for an Irish Diva to confront the Italian operatic establishment.

The Irish soprano, Veronica Dunne, described the impressive dedication which had to accompany an innate talent:

> For an Irish soprano to command operatic limelight during a politically sensitive time in virtually every prestigious opera house in Italy was an incredible achievement. Even in later years, for a foreigner, even one as famous as Callas, to break the closed-shop environment was a daunting undertaking – sheer will power, vocal excellence, personality and presence – ensured Peggie's success where so many had failed before and since.

By 1953 Margaret Sheridan was in retirement. The fairytale career that had scaled the Olympus of La Scala was over and her exacting standards had found a new focus on the people who surrounded her. The Shelbourne staff found that their supporting roles became more far onerous when Miss Sheridan was in town. As a perfectionist, she could compete with the redoubtable Margaret Cotton Jury and even the most cynical and seasoned in the waiter's dressing room dreaded her arrival.

Gabriel had only been working in the hotel for a few months when she returned to her regular room, number 507. On the following morning her breakfast was left to congeal on its tray while the waiters on duty bickered over it. Nobody was willing to brave a confrontation with the difficult Diva:

> Serving her meals was like going to court and proving you didn't commit a crime.

Inevitably the new boy drew the short straw and set off apprehensively with the tray. When his knock went unanswered he admitted himself in to the room with a passkey and was surprised to find the room apparently empty. As he looked around uncertainly a woman's head rose from the floor on the far side of the bed. Backstairs gossip had prepared him to expect any excess of eccentricity in Miss Burke Sheridan so he proffered her the breakfast on the floor, where she was, in fact, retrieving a lost lipstick. Instead of flying into one of her feared and famous rages she began to laugh. It was the start of an unusual friendship which was to last until she died in 1958.

After that morning Gabriel, at her request, served all her meals and while he did so they talked. Within weeks she knew every small detail of his life and family and recognised the essential loneliness that is the paradox of large, cramped families.

'You are an orphan like me', she told him. Few people realised that professional success had never assuaged her feeling of solitude. Even in retirement, she was a gallant performer. Noel Sheehan, who operated the Shelbourne's temperamental hydraulic lift remembers how, every day, on her descent from room 507, she would check her make up in the mirror, sling her fox fur over her shoulder and draw herself up to make a grand entrance into the lobby. Her queenly progress, nodding to right and left, led her through the revolving doors to the Green and she would disappear, nobody knew whither, until it was time to return and preside as *genus loci* of the five o'clock drawing room. Then, once installed in her regular seat in the left hand rear corner she would survey the field, summoning old friends like the equally flamboyant Michael McLiammór for audible and often outrageous repartee. Occasionally she would play the piano and sing. Her presence could never be overlooked. Her witty reminiscences of old friendships with musical luminaries such as Toscanini, Respighi, Puccini, Marconi, Lauri Volpi and Gigli ensured that she was a fascinating raconteur. An interview in *The Bell* in 1942 summed up her conversational style:

> Never did expert card-men nearing the end of a railway journey flash out their kings, queens and aces with such dexterity as La Sheridan flashes out the celebrities.

Acting the part of the ex-Diva had, in fact, become a grim charade in a retirement which was, initially, far from prosperous. Her resources, during the forties, were meagre. Royalties from recordings were negligible and her trademark couture outfits were carefully preserved relics from days gone by. Although she slept in the Shelbourne, she frequently ate economically and alone at the nearby modest Monument Café, long since gone.

Dame Margaret Burke Sheridan.

The dubious benefits of Inchicore street wisdom and an implacable, pious mother enabled Gabriel Walsh to recognise the insecurity beneath the singer's eccentricities. Her constant carping had a positive motive. Having worked so relentlessly to build her own career she found sloppy standards intolerable. In retirement she applied her formidable energies to re-educating and improving her fellow countrymen.

Her solitary struggle to maintain appearances was alleviated in the early fifties when a chance encounter became her salvation. She made the acquaintance of Ruth and Emerson Axe, a wealthy New York couple with a passion for opera. They quickly became intimate friends and patrons and did everything possible to ease her financial difficulties. From then on she was able to travel and live in comfort. Ruth Axe went to extraordinary lengths to gratify the whims of her friend and protégée. From 1951 to 1957 the Axe Castle in Tarrytown, above the Hudson river became Margaret Burke Sheridan's American home. It has been compared in style and scale to Lismore Castle, with forty five enormous rooms and a dining hall that could accommodate a hundred guests. The hundred acre estate, including a fine arboretum, and magnificent gardens, was a fitting setting for an operatic supernova.

Even so the martinet who could terrorise the Shelbourne staff found plenty to criticise in Tarrytown. The staff there aroused her ire as readily as their Irish counterparts. A wing of the house, specially designated for her use, had to be completely refurbished to conform with her taste. Even after that, lengthy sojourns in Tarrytown bored her. Every detail of her travel arrangements were handled by the Axes, who ensured that she would never again suffer financial anxiety.

At the time when Margaret Burke Sheridan met Gabriel Walsh she was probably enjoying the most consistent material security that she had ever known. She had never been selfish and an impulse of generosity led her to share her good fortune with the young commis. Some weeks after she returned to plague the Shelbourne her patroness, Mrs Axe, joined her there. Gabriel Walsh tells how he was standing outside Bewley's in Grafton Street enjoying the modest, free entertainment of watching a man grinding coffee on the other side of the plate glass window. Since he was off-duty he was wearing the clothes which his mother had procured in the Iveagh Market, a distinctly downmarket outlet which specialised in the garments of dead paupers:

> I was watching the man at the coffee machine in Bewleys when I saw her reflection in the window. A big black hat with a feather sticking out of it appeared and descended on the window like a large bird coming out of

> the sky. The image was unmistakable. She was standing behind me holding the arm of another woman. I felt a mixture of shock and embarrassment and wondered if she'd recognise me out of my waiter's outfit. I didn't look the same when I was off duty.

She did recognise him and the mortified, shabby teenager was duly presented to Mrs Axe. In spite of his efforts to escape the two ladies strolled down Grafton Street with him, stopping off at a gentleman's outfitters to equip him with new clothes from head to toe. It was his first but not his last encounter with Ruth Axe's generosity. Soon after that, at the prompting of Miss Burke Sheridan, the Axes proposed themselves as Gabriel's guardians and asked his mother's permission to take him to America. Within a year of finding a job at the Shelbourne the commis from Inchicore, who had braved the terrors of room 507, was living in the castle of Emerson Wirt Axe, descendant of the first Attorney General of the United States under the tutelage of Mrs Axe and Margaret Burke Sheridan.

His life had changed so dramatically that it was almost traumatic. He went back to school, driving himself there in his own car and taking his part in the gilded life of young WASP America. He did not revisit Ireland until 1970. By then his life had taken a few more unexpected twists.

At the time when he was expected to enter the Axes' world of Wall Street finance, another chance encounter had changed his career. In a New York bar one day he met a young actor on his way to an audition. They hit it off well enough for Gabriel, who up to then had entertained no thespian ambitions, to tag along. Both of them were cast in a production of Shakespeare's *Troilus and Cressida* and both had good notices from the critics. The new acquaintance was called Robert Redford. Gabriel later made the transition from actor to screen writer. When he returned to the Shelbourne in 1970, entering the doors to register as a guest, he was there to make a film. His screenplay *Quackser Fortune has a Cousin in the Bronx* was to be shot in Dublin and he was accompanied by the two lead actors, Gene Wilder and Margot Kidder, who later played Lois Lane in *Superman.* The tattered movie magazines which had been his dream fodder in Inchicore had been translated into reality. The script was nominated by the Writers Guild of America as the best written American screen comedy of that year.

The main character, Quackser Fortune, a peddler of horse manure, rendered obsolete by the advent of motorised lorries, was authentic Inchicore. The filming process was pure Hollywood. The polar opposites of Gabriel's early life had found a sort of resolution. Today, dividing his time between New York and his home on the Blackwater near Fermoy he still believes that Margaret Burke Sheridan was the catalyst that changed his life.

When she died, another member of the Shelbourne staff became a beneficiary of her good will. Noel Sheehan was left a small bequest. The old hydraulic lift in the hotel was as temperamental as any Diva and required careful handling. Noel was the lift operator who had piloted her most securely down from 507 to make her grand entrances into the lobby.

It was fitting that someone like Noel should be remembered with gratitude. He, Jimmy Dixon and their colleagues manning the porters' desk were the front line of the Shelbourne operation. Everybody arriving or leaving filtered through their hands and their task was to ensure that the dignity and good humour of the establishment were not disrupted. That demanded constant vigilance and tact and when security became a serious concern, during the seventies, their responsibilities became even more onerous.

Celebrities, arriving in increasing numbers in the fifties, had to be protected from over-eager fans. Hunting guests, the backbone of the winter business, were charged with raw vitality by constant exercise. They needed errands run by day and night and endless valeting to be organised, but, with the passage of time even the keenest sportsmen could decline into doddery old regulars and require more delicate services.

People like Lord Fingall, in his later years, needed a gentle steer to keep on course. He would arrive in town early in the morning clutching an *aide memoire* listing the business which he was to transact at Leverett and

Fry, Smyths of the Green, Drummonds Seeds, Mitchell's Wine Merchants and so forth. He would start his day in town with a visit to John Conroy, the Shelbourne's permanent barber, and depart, spruced up, to do his business, returning frequently to the hotel to recuperate between calls. The errands always seemed to take an age. One day he reappeared in the barbers at three in the afternoon and asked for a haircut. Conroy reminded him that his hair had been cut only that morning. The peer dug his list from his pocket and perused it. 'Impossible,' he declared, 'It isn't crossed off.' It was obvious that if he did not remember to erase each call as he made it he would simply repeat the whole procedure. After that, tactful hands at the front desk would delete his business as it was done and he would return home with a tranquil mind.

Elderly patrons could always rely on the Shelbourne staff and many of them were appreciative. John Cornelius Sullivan of County Meath, an eccentric and reclusive hotel resident of thirty years standing, left £2,000 in 'tips' when he died in the early forties. Lift operators, valets, cashiers, receptionists, secretaries, telephonists, porters, chambermaids, and waiters shared the bonanza. Another long term hotel resident, Frank Sheedy and Colonel Jury both received £500 and Barney Molloy was left £200. The largest legacy, reported to be £800, was left to Patrick Kelly, the third floor valet, who had postponed his holidays to look after the needs of the ailing ninety-three year old.

Patrick Kelly's services were rewarded as generously as they were given but sometimes the favours requited from management carried a risk of diminishing returns.

The executive role, keeping both sides of the green baize door on an even keel, was no sinecure, and could be awkward when names from *Burkes* and *Debretts* became names in *Stubbs.* Maintaining goodwill without bankrupting the business required a pragmatic blend of sympathy and scepticism.

In *My Ireland,* Kate O'Brien lauded 'the dear tolerant Shelbourne'. There were occasions when it was almost too tolerant for its own good. Kate O'Brien's visits to the Shelbourne from her Connemara home in Roundstone would have brought her into contact with Bernard Molloy who was one of the hotel's best known personalities, arriving as manager in 1937 and remaining there until his death in 1962. As a racing man, the high spot of his week was his Saturday excursion to the race course with his friend, Frank Sheedy, who had been permanently resident in the Shelbourne since the death of his wife. A thick file of bad debtors surviving from his days in management attests to his readiness to take a gamble on an outsider. His previous post at White's of Wexford had, perhaps, not prepared him for the gilt-edged chicanery which he would encounter in the capital. When it came to negotiating reduced terms or helping out straitened clients he was a notoriously soft touch.

Peter Maguire, S.C. solicited a loan one evening in 1950. He and a friend had completed their first year as devilling barristers and brought their Master out for cocktails in the Shelbourne Rooms to be followed by dinner at Dublin Airport. In those days, when air travel still exuded glamour it was the *dernier cri* of sophistication to drive out to Collinstown and feast in an ambience of AvGas and whining propellers. When Maguire and his colleague came to pay the bar bill in the Shelbourne before leaving for dinner they discovered that neither of them had remembered to transfer their wallet into their evening clothes. They took their predicament to Bernard Molloy who loaned them sufficient to cover drinks and dinner without demur, even though they were dining in a competing establishment. On that occasion, he was repaid promptly but at other times he was less fortunate. In the days before plastic credit cards, cheques frequently shared the properties of rubber and there were always cads and bounders willing to bounce them. Appearances could be deceptive, too. Even a dog collar was no guarantee of fiscal probity. A surprising number of men of the cloth, of both denominations, figure in Molloy's file of debtors.

At the start of Horse Show Week in 1951 a party of owners and trainers checked in. They had been at Goodwood for the races and it had clearly been a hilarious week. Among the party was an Egyptian gentleman, clearly an intimate and trusted friend. Molloy, as a racing enthusiast himself, had a soft spot for the owners and trainers who frequented the Shelbourne for race meetings and bloodstock sales. On their recommendation he accepted an IOU from the Egyptian in exchange for a personal loan of £50. A week of boisterous partying, characteristic of the

Shelbourne in Horse Show Week, ensued. The exotic foreigner was the life and soul of the glamorous group, hosting the heavyweights of the bloodstock industry.

Bernard Molloy

'He was in with all the Horse Show Week crowd', Molloy reported sadly in a later report to his directors. 'On 9 August he gave a dinner party, the bill being £14 odd and on 12 August another party, the bill amounting to £17 odd. He tipped lavishly and was in dinner dress with a white coat and seemed to be one of the party on all occasions.' On Sunday he left – to go to Tramore races saying that he would settle up his account on his return and instructing Molloy to reserve a plane seat for his departure the following Monday.

The lavish tips, which were, after all Molloy's own money must have added insult to injury. The outstanding account owed to the hotel amounted to £39/7/10. When the Manager was first assailed by doubt he recalled, 'I asked – (one of the racing set) who exactly he was and he said he thought he was alright but later came and told me that he might or might not be alright.'

It transpired, eventually, that the racegoers had picked him up in the bar at Goodwood the previous week. None of them had ever seen him before. High on the adrenaline and alcohol of race week they had insisted that their new acquaintance accompany them back to Dublin for the fun of the Horse Show. Sobering up, after two solid weeks on the tear, they agreed unanimously that they had suspected he was a bit fishy from the start. This was cold comfort for Mr Molloy, who had been stung for £50 from his own pocket and was now obliged to explain a hefty outstanding account to his Directors. Earlier that year he had been forced to cope with the chaos of the bank strike which had probably left the Shelbourne, like everybody else, with more outstanding debts than usual.

Even by the open-handed standards of Horse Show week the Egyptian's consumption had been prodigal. The basic charges for his stay were standard. His apartment (including baths) was twenty-five shillings per night at the start of his stay, dropping to seventeen shillings and sixpence later. These rates had changed little over the years. During the high season in 1926 superior rooms with private bath, light and attendance were twenty-two shillings and sixpence and the rate remained the same in the Blue Guide for 1949.

As it was August, the Egyptian visitor had no charges for fires which would have cost him another two or three shillings per day, nor did he have a dog with him which would have incurred an additional daily charge of half a crown. Personal hygiene does not seem to have been a high priority for him either. His laundry costs were a negligible seven shillings and eight pence and he spent eight shillings and eight pence on telephone calls. The remaining £32/9 had been consumed in food and drink, only one shilling of which was spent on tea or coffee.

Mr Molloy's concern is understandable. His correspondence to debtors pointed out repeatedly that his Directors held him responsible for overdue accounts. If this was indeed the case his net loss was only a few shillings short of £90, a serious sum to lose. The wages records show that, at that time, first year commis waiters were getting £1/6 net per week. Three years later Gabriel Walsh started on the same amount. Experienced veterans of the dining room and coffee room averaged around about three pounds and Carroll, the senior coffee room waiter was on an enviable £5/18/4. The hotel's resident french polisher, a skilled craftsman, was earning £3/13/10 per week and the boiler man, one of the most important functionaries in the establishment netted six pounds, sixteen shillings and eleven pence.

There is no record of Bernard Molloy's salary but he was definitely not earning anything approaching the £3,000 per annum which a High Court judge commanded at that time. In 1950, Monsieur de La Rochefoucauld had written from Paris to Peter Jury about a new chef:

> On the other hand, I should point out that we find your proposed salary of £ 200 per annum rather low. We have often noticed that those employees who go abroad feel they are entitled at least to the same salaries as they would have in France. In your particular case, everyone believes that in Dublin salaries are about the same as in England.
>
> For your information, in France such men would receive monthly around £ 30. As you add the lodging, I believe that a salary of about £ 275 a year would suit them.

A bad debt of £90, therefore, was not to be taken lightly. As suspicion resonated through the Shelbourne that the miscreant was still carousing with the more resilient survivors of Goodwood and the Horse Show Week down at the Tramore races. Molloy telephoned the Grand Hotel Tramore and was given breezy reassurances. Not only would the debt be cleared, another member of the party had the money in his pocket at that very moment. Down the line that allegation caused more confusion. The courier was to prove, at best, absent-minded.

A racegoer, returning wearily to the Shelbourne at the end of the week reported that the Egyptian, realising no doubt that the game was up in Ireland, had made a hasty departure for Belgium. Molloy initiated some detective work with Aer Lingus but the debtor's name did not figure on any of their passenger lists. It later transpired that he had travelled in style in a privately chartered plane, no doubt paid for by another note of hand.

Molloy pursued him doggedly through London, Brighton, Rome and Cairo. In the course of the year, over forty letters were filed. By September Molloy was in correspondence with the Royal Egyptian Consulate General:

> ... We understand this gentleman is connected with horse racing and is fairly well known in Cairo. We got his address as c/o Gezirah Sporting Club but the letter which we wrote was returned to us. I would be grateful if you could be of any assistance in this matter as I am held personally responsible for the account.

The political instability of Egypt at that time muddied the waters even more. In October a letter arrived from the shameless debtor:

> Forward your bill to the Excelsior in Rome – to await arrival. I am going to North Italy for a long rest after a very serious accident which occurred to me in Turkey.

Molloy returned his serve:

> I am placed in a very awkward position with my Directors as I have been in serious trouble for allowing this account to be left unpaid – I have been compelled to guarantee this account myself.

In December the manager of the Hotel Excelsior entered the picture:

> I wish to inform you that this person has never come here and that your two letters, together with a letter of the Hotel Metropole in Brighton and one of the Hotel Ritz in London are still lying in our Post Office unclaimed.

That month the Egyptian resurfaced in the Gezira Club in Cairo. Molloy pleaded:

> I have been compelled to make this money good.

At the same time he confided to the manager of the Metropole in Brighton:

> ... like yourself we are doubtful of the gentleman but we are hoping for the best.

During February a member of the horsey set, who had already cleared the £50 loan, remembered to hand over a further £5 which the Egyptian gentleman had asked him to return to Molloy the previous August. The amended account was still outstanding when Horse Show week came around again. Worse still, another member of the Gezira Club was already heading for the Shelbourne accompanied by an entire Egyptian Bridge team. At that point Molloy handed over the position of manager to Dennis McGeary and became the Shelbourne's first public relations officer. As a racing man he was probably relieved that in future his punting could be confined to nothing more risky than the horses.

Dennis McGeary had been working in London. Even so, he must have been impressed by the cosmopolitan guest list in Dublin's Shelbourne. It was beginning to looking increasingly like the cast of a Cecil B. de Mille epic. James Cagney, Maureen O'Hara, John Wayne, Stan Laurel, Oliver Hardy, Elizabeth Taylor, Richard Burton, Rock Hudson, Burl Ives, Orson Welles, Robert Taylor and Rita Hayworth, accompanied by her husband Aly Khan were some of the screen personalities who came to stay.

In 1953 royalty appeared too, in the substantial form of Queen Salote of Tonga who booked in with Princess Mataoho and a large entourage including two personal cooks, on her way home from the coronation of Queen Elizabeth in London. The expansive Queen Salote had won instant popularity with the British public. Her genial, twenty-three stone presence made her easily recognisable among the cloned foreign dignitaries and she was one of the few people attending the ceremonies who looked as though she was actually enjoying it. In the State procession from Westminster Abbey she filled most of her open carriage, her waving arm obscuring most of the slight, elaborately uniformed man who had been inserted at her side. It is said that Noel Coward, when asked to opine whether Queen Salote's escort was her Prime Minister or merely an ADC, replied laconically, 'Neither. That's her lunch.'

Dennis McGeary was given just three days notice to procure a bed which would accommodate the antipodean monarch in comfort and safety. There was nothing in the hotel or, indeed, the city that matched

Queen Salote of Tonga

the specifications sent by the Queen's courtiers so his first challenge was finding a craftsman who could make the gigantic bed within three days. Amazingly that was achieved. The next challenge was getting it installed in the royal suite. Jimmy Dixon and Noel Sheehan remember the contortions and ingenuity required to wrestle the mammoth base up the back stairs to room 217 in time for the Queen's arrival. She spent two nights in it. Mr and Mrs Sullivan from Wellington, New Zealand were allocated the royal apartment the following night. They must have been mightily impressed by the grand scale of their sleeping accommodation.

Some five years later an American couple who had been married during coronation year occupied the Tonga suite. They were John and Jacqueline Kennedy. He had been an unsuccessful contestant for the

American Vice Presidency in 1956 and was, at the time of that Irish visit, campaigning for the Presidency. The rest is history.

The Tonga Suite, as it became known to the staff, and the suite adjoining it in 215 and 216 were the hotel's premier accommodation in those days. Most of the dignitaries who used them, such as Pierre Trudeau or Harold Wilson were far too discreet to leave anecdotes behind them. The occupants who finally carried off the title of 'Most Lively in the Tonga' were Peter O'Toole and Donal McCann, who used the suite during their run of *Waiting for Godot* at the Abbey Theatre.

A more dubious distinction was awarded to Barbara Rush and Rock Hudson. Miss Rush stayed in the suite for four months while filming *Captain Lightfoot* and her co-star occupied room 316 on the floor above. During their stay, the staff allocated to look after them gave the best of service, staying on late and coming in early. When the film was finished they were summoned to 217 to receive a parting gift. Up to that point, neither Rush nor Hudson had crossed anybody's palm with silver so the staff went upstairs with high hopes. Each of them was presented with a signed photograph of the stars, who were, from then on, considered the Shelbourne's meanest tippers.

A less noticeable guest, resident at the time of Queen Salote's visit was the novelist Edwin O'Connor from Boston. He lived in the hotel for several months that year, working in his room each morning and spending the afternoons with friends and fellow writers such as Seán Ó'Faoláin, Frank O'Connor, Roger McHugh and Conor Cruise O'Brien.

The Last Hurrah, the book which he wrote in the Shelbourne during that period, deals with Boston Irish political life and became a bestseller after its publication in 1958. Spencer Tracy starred in the film version which was made two years later.

O'Connor's biographer, Professor Charles Duffy of Providence College, Rhode Island, tells us that O'Connor was a regular springtime visitor to the Shelbourne for many years:

> He almost always left Boston for Ireland, either on St Patrick's Day or the day before. Seems he was

> embarrassed about the rather tawdry shenanigans in Boston on St Paddy's day, especially since he associated more with the Yankees of Beacon Hill than with the local Irish. Apparently he preferred the (then) quieter celebrations in Dublin.

It is unlikely that the decorous atmosphere of the Shelbourne was disrupted by the sort of hooley that Mr O'Connor fled in Boston but that does not indicate a deficiency of patriotism. In spite of its aspirations to internationalism, the Shelbourne had always sold itself as, primarily, an Irish hotel. The shamrock, so inextricably entwined with the semiotics of St Patrick's Day, and all things Irish had been registered as the Shelbourne's trade mark since 18 August 1898.

CHAPTER EIGHT

'THIS RENTIER HEAVEN OF RACING CHAPS'

The Permissive Society was far too sexy to catch on in Catholic Ireland. Nowadays the innocent iconoclasm of the swinging sixties seems almost naive but at that time the more colourful aspects of its culture were kept well off shore. However, the optimism of the era was contagious and prosperity and confidence blossomed here from the very start of the decade. Northern problems appeared to be in remission, at least until 1968. The new republic, established by Costello's repeal of the External Relations Act, was just twelve years old and embarking on an independent adolescence. The Whitaker Plan, instituted in 1958, was working even better than had been projected. GDP was growing like a bean sprout, interest rates were low and there was a building boom. The population of Ireland had become consumers.

For the Shelbourne, especially, 1960 initiated a new phase. The tenure of the Cotton Jury family, which had lasted for nearly a century, was coming to an end. The hotel had been registered first as a private company in 1927. In 1950 it had become a public company with a board still composed mainly of congenial Cotton Jury family connections. By 1960 it had reverted to being a private company as all its issued share capital had been acquired by a parent company, namely the British group Trust Houses. The Shelbourne Hotel Limited was now a shell company with no assets of its own. On November 7 Colonel Edward Jury, received a letter from Sir Geoffrey Crowther of Trust Houses:

> I have been out of London for a week and have therefore only just seen your note of October 26th. It gives me the greatest pleasure to know that you feel happy about the change of ownership of the Shelbourne. I can well understand that this was a very difficult decision for you and your family to take and I can give you the fullest assurances that we shall attempt to run it in a way that is in keeping with its traditions. We regard your son as being one of the best assets that we have acquired through this transaction and I look forward to many years of co-operation with him.

Peter Jury, making the transition from heir to asset, as a forty-one year-old family man might have had some apprehensions but, as an officer and a gentleman he kept them hidden. He was, in fact, no stranger to intimations of anxiety with regard to the family business. His father, Colonel Edward Jury, had never been an easy taskmaster. He was a typical British Raj Sahib barking out orders, an anachronism in a post-colonial world and an impediment to a modern business.

As early as 1949, only two years after taking over the management of the Shelbourne, Peter Jury had appended a postscript to a routine letter of business to his cousin and fellow director C.E. Wrangham:

> My father has decided that he will not go over for the General Meeting this year. I have not unduly encouraged him to change his mind.

The Colonel's retirement from active management had never relieved the premises of his fierce, bewhiskered presence. His habit of treating the staff like a battalion of Gurkhas did not improve with age. In fact, his eccentricities increased. As a septuagenarian he was still a prodigious consumer of whiskey. He developed disquieting habits as his drinking day progressed. One of his favourite ploys was to ring a bell for a top up, then run away, watch in hand, to hide and log the waiter's response time. He had given good service to the family business but, like his grandmother, the redoubtable Margaret, he had reached his sell-by date.

Geoffrey Crowther was Chairman of the Trust Houses, a large organisation, owning a chain of inns and catering outlets throughout England. The company had developed from the Hertford Public House Trust established by the fourth Earl Grey in 1903. In a document circulated on 30 September 1960, shareholders had been offered the option to exchange cumulative preference shares of Shelbourne stock for par value of Trust House stock. Ordinary shareholders were given the chance to make a nominal profit by exchanging 100 ordinary shares of five shillings each in the Shelbourne for 45 £1 shares in Trust House.

Sir Geoffrey, later Lord, Crowther

The Shelbourne Directors, C.E. Wrangham Esq., Captain P.C. Jury, Colonel E.C. Jury, Lieutenant-Colonel T.A.E. Cairnes, Prince J-L de Faucigny Lucinge, Sir George E.J. Mahon and General Sir Nevil Brownjohn were unanimous in their recommendations that the shareholders should accept the offer. They did. The change of ownership made few immediate differences to the surface rhythms of the hotel. Amongst the extensive holdings of Trust House the Shelbourne was, at that stage, the most significant single acquisition in the company's portfolio. The composition of the Board of Trust House (Ireland) reflected this fact. It was a modified version of the original Shelbourne Board with Peter Jury as chairman. He also continued to be managing director of the hotel and the management team remained, initially, unchanged.

Trust House would subsequently acquire other Irish hotels, including Acton's Hotel in Kinsale, the International Hotel in Killarney, the Royal

Hibernian Hotel in Dublin and the Old Ground in Ennis. An Irish holding company, Tara Holdings, became their vehicle for business here for a while but later reverted to Trust Houses (Ireland). The concern over possibility that the new arrangements might cause problems further down the line was, in 1960, outweighed for most by the positive advantages.

In January 1961 Ralph Cotton's son-in-law, Cuthbert Wrangham, who preferred, understandably, to be known as Dennis, circulated a letter to the members of the former Shelbourne Board. His own retirement from it had been marked by a handsome presentation of £823 in savings certificates for each of his five children:

> What history the Shelbourne has made in the hands of these two families over almost half a century. For a small fraction of that period I had the honour to be titular head of that team that led the hotel out of war-time difficulties to its present state. This was the work of a team – not any one person, least of all myself. Most credit must go to Peter Jury whose singular flair for décor, whose patience pertinacity and sense of humour made all our plans triumphantly successful. Nor will any one of us ever forget how much was due to the commonsense and warm humanity of Tom Cairnes. The end of it all, quickly as it had to come, has brought much to be thankful for – a fair price, a new owner of high repute and excellent prospects for Peter and his staff.

His covering letter to his cousin Peter was less airbrushed:

> Times were pretty grim when you first appeared on the scene and I regarded you as a gift from heaven...
>
> Why you did not go mad under the combined strain of dealing with the Shelbourne Hotel when nearly on the rocks and with me, I shall never know. In fact, however, the rehabilitation of the Shelbourne took place and was really something of a miracle. We both contributed ideas but you many more: and you had to execute them!

> I have always greatly admired your taste which seems to me for some inexplicable reason very seldom to go wrong. I hope and think it will be all the more stimulating and interesting for you now that the scope can become so much bigger.

The old days had not been all plain sailing and change was greeted with optimism. Glamour was abroad and some reverberations of romance penetrated to the Shelbourne. One of the world's most attractive couples, Prince Rainier of Monaco and his wife, Princess Grace, initiated a regular relationship with the Shelbourne. At that time the premier suite in the hotel was still the 'Tonga' suite in rooms 217 and 218 and the adjacent apartments in 214 and 215. The Grimaldis formed an attachment to the view of St Stephen's Green from room 270, which became their regular allocation, and is now known as the Princess Grace Suite. Their sojourns were uneventful and dignified. Unlike James Cagney who danced on the piano in the drawing room, or Stan Laurel, who had to retain the services of Jimmy Dixon, the porter, to extract him from armchairs, they generated no salty stories. Their time here was generally arranged so that the Princess could spend some time with her friend, the late Joan FitzGerald (Mrs Garret FitzGerald). The two would chat quietly in a corner. The staff remember her with affection as a person who was invariably courteous to them and tolerant of an intrusive public.

John F. Kennedy, who had stayed in 217 with his wife, Jacqueline, during his campaign for the Presidential nomination in 1958, returned on an official visit in June 1963. The return of a Wexford emigrant's grandson as President of the United States engendered possessive pride throughout the country. The news of his assassination in Dallas only a few months later was felt as a personal bereavement by many. His photograph was displayed alongside that of Pope John XXIII in many Irish homes.

A more familial loss for the Shelbourne occurred the year after President Kennedy's death when the Honourable Tara Browne died in a car crash, at the age of twenty-one. Since his earliest childhood he had been a familiar figure in the hotel, coming on visits to town with his brother, Garech, and his mother, Lady Oranmore and Browne, one of the Shelbourne's most glamorous patrons. During the summer the Browne children rarely wore shoes. Tourists were surprised to see barefoot children alighting from a gleaming, chauffeur-driven Rolls Royce at the entrance to the hotel. During the late fifties the family moved into the Shelbourne for a while when their house was damaged by a fire. Tara Browne was a sixties icon, a golden-haired archetype of the decade's gilded youth, who featured prominently in the social columns. He seemed to have a charmed life but it ended prematurely in an accident in the King's Road, swinging London's epicentre. The song, 'A Day in the Life', which the Beatles wrote and recorded on their *Sgt Pepper* album is a poignant epitaph on his untimely death.

At the time of Tara Browne's death, his brother Garech had already done much to change international perceptions of Irish music. With his friend, Dr Ivor Browne and others, including the poet John Montague, he had founded Claddagh Records as a conduit to bring traditional music to a wider public. It seems scarcely credible, now that the genre has achieved international recognition, that it was a minority interest in those days. No market-driven international record company had been prepared to risk investing in such an arcane area. A shared passion inspired this group of under-capitalised young men to establish Claddagh Records. The company's first L.P, featuring Leo Rowsome, the uilleann piper, was released in 1959. The label went on to become the definitive vehicle for a Irish musicians and composers, ranging from the Chieftains to John Field. Claddagh secured the survival of a musical heritage, which was in danger of being devalued.

Derek Mahon (photo Sarah Owens).

The Shelbourne provided the venue for meeting and planning the new company and its developments during the early days. Seán Ó Riada, who was profoundly important to the company's development was a *habitué* of the hotel and the Claddagh Spoken Word list would, in time, include many regulars from the Horseshoe Bar, such as Patrick Kavanagh, Seamus Heaney, John Montague, Derek Mahon, Liam O'Flaherty and Jack McGowran.

The idea of forming the Chieftains, Claddagh's best known performers, grew out of discussions on the aims and development of the company. Paddy Moloney, the group's leader had been a founder member of Seán Ó Riada's 'folk orchestra', Ceoltóirí Cualainn, which was launched with a concert in the Shelbourne ballroom. On the eve of the debut the orchestra still had no name. Ó Riada had a last minute brain-storming session with Seán Mac Reamoinn. Ó Riada's house was situated close to an ancient thoroughfare called Cualan's way and they came up with the idea of calling the group Ceoltóirí Cualainn meaning Cualann's musicians.

Seán Ó Riada, signing the score of Hercules Dux Ferrariae at the Shelbourne.

However arbitrary the title, the folk orchestra's blend of nostalgia, romance and modernity generated immediate enthusiasm with the public. Ó Riada was then the musical director of the Abbey Theatre and had achieved wide popular success with his score for the film *Mise Éire.* Garech Browne defines him as 'the single most constructive influence on the new perception of Irish music at that time.'

This re-invigoration of a people's art form in Ireland was in tune with cultural shifts elsewhere. Western art was becoming democratised. New York's Greenwich Village and London's Kings' Road had usurped the more élitist ateliers of Paris. Blue-collar artists were emerging and harbingers of change were perceptible even in the Dublin of the late fifties. Brendan Behan was typical of the new breed. His background and personal history was tailor-made for success in contemporary London or New York.

In January 1957 Iain Hamilton, editorial director of Hutchinson, checked into the Shelbourne. The previous year Valentine Iremonger, the poet and diplomat had commended an incomplete manuscript by the then relatively unknown Behan. Hamilton was sufficiently interested to come to Dublin to make his own assessment. Unfortunately, his arrival at the Shelbourne was announced in *The Irish Times,* attracting an avalanche of unsolicited manuscripts. Then, as now, the possibility of a contract with a major British publishing house could persuade even the most militantly republican writers to overcome their xenophobia. While Hamilton searched for Behan throughout the city, other writers' offerings piled up in his hotel room.

He was sitting in the Shelbourne lobby two days after his arrival when Behan rambled in looking, as usual, like an unmade bed. His wife Beatrice was with him and he was carrying a tattered briefcase containing the manuscript. Hamilton was well aware of the first impression that he himself must have made on the writer:

> A bloody Presbyterian Scots chancer on the make, too neatly dressed, with a moustache a little too British military for comfort …

A typical Shelbourne patron, in fact. Behan, on the other hand, was scruffy, unshaven and faintly musty at close quarters. In the days of Mrs

Cotton Jury he would never have been allowed through the door, but draughts of change were pervading even the smug complacency of the Shelbourne. Hamilton's first impressions disregarded the superficial grime and tipsiness:

Brendan Behan.

> Whatever else he was, Behan was God-branded. I don't know how else to put it. Among other odours, that of sanctity was predominant. It might have been Coleridge's mariner who was talking to me.

A six-hour drinking session ensued. Later, sitting up in his bed in the Shelbourne, Hamilton read the thirty-page start of the manuscript he had come to find and saw the beginning of something extraordinary. Behan signed a contract with Hutchinsons in the Shelbourne and promptly set about drinking the generous, initial advance of £350. It required a long hard struggle on Hamilton's part to get the completed manuscript of *Borstal Boy* delivered in time for its London launch late the following year.

When the book was banned in Ireland and later in Australia and New Zealand, Behan took Swiftian revenge in satire and went round the Dublin pubs singing, to the tune of 'MacNamara's Band':

> My name is Brendan Behan, I'm the latest of the banned
> Although we're small in numbers we're the best banned in the land,
> We're read at wakes and weddin's and in every parish hall,
> And under library counters sure you'll have no trouble at all.

He probably sang it in the Shelbourne too, for in the year that *Borstal Boy* was published the newly opened Horseshoe Bar had established an enduring place on Dublin's drinking map. Behan was one of many writers and media people who took to its womb-like ambience like a duck to water. It was less formal than the Shelbourne Rooms and far more hygienic than the average pub. One stifling summer afternoon the actress, Siobhán McKenna, made an entrance. In tones as sultry as the weather she begged the barman to suggest something long and cold. Behan from the far side of the bar bawled, 'Give her a Polar bear's prick.'

The Reading and Writing Room, which was to become the Horseshoe Bar

The Horseshoe Bar had formerly been the Reading and Writing Room with a curving staircase on the far side leading to the Shelbourne Rooms. A brief incarnation as a television room had not been a great success and on occasions the area had been pressed into service as a temporary bar. Peter Jury and his banqueting manager Padraic Browne had the idea of converting it permanently into an intimate but sophisticated cocktail bar. They commissioned a design from Aidan Prior who was then managing the Brown Thomas contract interior department. He had just recently engaged the services of Sam Stephenson, a newly graduated architect from Bolton Street, as a consultant to the Brown Thomas team and the pair set about creating a bar which was so successful that hardly a detail of the design has ever been altered. The stairs were removed and the two large south-facing windows were impenetrably shuttered by wooden louvered blinds. Between them a concealed pantry area was constructed. The soft interior lighting never altered by day or night, creating a clubby, cosy atmosphere in total contrast to the hotel's airy public rooms. Time and season in the Horseshoe are still best marked by the diurnal rhythms of the regular barflies. It has been described as an ideal place for men without a future to meet women with a past.

Forty-one years later it is unchanged in appearance and popularity. The sole alteration over the years has been a variation of the dark background colours. The original wine red was replaced first by forest green and, in 1998 by navy blue. That any fifties interior should stand the test of time so well is an eloquent endorsement for Prior and Stephenson's ability to combine contemporary fashion with enduring taste. For Aidan Prior this talent ensured that his own shop, Prior Interiors, would remain Dublin's most prestigious furniture store for over thirty years. In Sam Stephenson's case it was the start of a distinguished career as one of the city's leading architects. Their collaboration in the Horseshoe Bar was entirely felicitous.

Scandinavian influences were strong in interior design in the late fifties. Architectural embellishments were ruthlessly excised and ceilings lowered to create the blandest possible space. Unusually for that period the original proportions of the room were retained and the fine plasterwork on the ceiling and walls was kept as a feature. An atmosphere of acceptable decadence was provided by the Hogarth prints of *The Rake's Progress* which ornament the pediment of the bar. Sam Stephenson was an enthusiastic admirer of William Hogarth and felt that the prints would be particularly appropriate. They proved elusive but, after a long search a set was obtained through Leo Smith's Dawson Gallery.

Recently four original drawings by the illustrator Paul Hogarth have been rediscovered in the hotel by Michael O'Sullivan. Paul Hogarth, a direct descendant of the earlier William, stayed in the Shelbourne for six months while working on the graphics for *Brendan Behan's Island*. It was a nightmare assignment for the illustrator whose eminence had made him accustomed to more co-operative authors. Behan was drinking heavily for the entire duration of the project. When Hogarth's work was completed he was disturbed to discover that there was still no accompanying text.

The equine theme of the Horseshoe Bar can only have contributed further to its popularity. Hunting, racing and Horse Show clientele had always been the backbone of the Shelbourne's business. Their names dot the registration books as punctually as daisies on a lawn. Some of the racing personalities included the Aga Khan, whose stallion Tulyar was sold to the Irish National Stud for a record price in 1953, Aly Khan, the McCalmonts of Mount Juliet, Joe and P.P. Hogan, Mrs Burke of Stackallen, Willie O'Grady, Paddy Sleator, Tom Dreaper, Captain Rogers, Martin Molony, Gordon Richards (whose son's wedding was held in the hotel) and 'Le Maestro', Lester Piggot, who believed that Irish racing followers were the most knowledgeable in the world.

The Duchess of Westminster, another frequent visitor, owned Arkle, one of the fastest steeplechasers of all time. He was the superhorse of the sixties, winning the Cheltenham Gold Cup in three consecutive years, starting in 1964, when he also won the Irish Grand National. He was so popular with the racing public that a special mail van had to be assigned to deliver his sacks of fan mail to Tom Dreaper's yard in Ashbourne.

Race meetings brought owners, trainers and riders alike to mingle in the Shelbourne. Some had been connected with the turf for generations, others were newcomers, like Charles Haughey who acquired his first racehorse in 1959. Almost all of them availed of the services of Jack Kelly, purveyor of transport and peace of mind to the equine fraternity. He managed, by some gift of ubiquity, to park everybody's car and drive them all to and from the races or the sales. He is remembered by many as an indispensable adjunct to any horsey business that had to be transacted in town.

For Vincent O'Brien, the trainer who dominated the sport for decades, the Shelbourne, and the Russell Hotel on the far side of the Green, were an integral part of the racing scene. As he told his biographer, Raymond Smith, 'If you did not meet some of your racing friends in one of them it was odds on that they would be in the other.' One Friday evening in 1951 O'Brien had a particularly memorable encounter in the Shelbourne. As he was racing at the Curragh the following day he planned a quiet, early dinner. He was having a pre-prandial bracer in the Shelbourne Bar when his friends Waring Willis and Gerry Annesley dropped in accompanied by an attractive girl who enjoyed the racing gossip. She was Jacqueline Wittenoom, from Australia, whose father was a member of parliament and had been Mayor of Albany in Western Australia for twenty years. The four ended up dining together and before the evening ended O'Brien's romantic fate was sealed. Six months later he and Jacqueline Wittenoom were married in the University Church and returned across the Green to the site of their first meeting to host a reception for four hundred people. The groomsmen included the O'Brien brothers, Phonsi and Dermot, Waring Willis who had introduced the couple, the bride's brother, Bob Wittenoom from Australia and the jockey, Martin Molony.

A three-times winner of the Irish Grand National Molony's versatility made him as great a racing legend as O'Brien. His genius lent itself equally to National Hunt and classic flat racing. In 1951 he made history by riding Silver Fame to victory in the Cheltenham Gold Cup and subsequently coming third in the Epsom Derby. Every famous rider seems in retrospect to be defined by one special mount. In Martin Molony's case this was probably the O'Brien-trained Hatton's Grace.

Jacqueline and Vincent O'Brien became engaged in Jammet's Restaurant, which was situated at the junction of Nassau Street and Grafton Street. Diners in Dublin's only truly French restaurant were cosseted in a *fin de siècle* Parisian atmosphere of sybaritic comfort. The food and service were excellent. The ambitiously conceived murals were of more doubtful quality but until its closure in 1967 it was unquestionably the city's smartest restaurant. After race meetings the place was packed with owners, trainers, riders and lucky punters. Returning racegoers who were less flush with cash were more likely to round off their day at the Dolphin in Essex Street, a restaurant famous for the excellence of its steaks and the frank functionality of its waiting staff. Hall porters Jimmy Dixon and Noel Sheehan can recall many evenings when O'Brien set off from the Shelbourne to celebrate a racing victory in Jammet's. When Cottage Rake won the first of three successive Gold Cups in 1948 the menu offered 'Le Saumon Fumé Churchtown, Le Potage de Vincent, Les Paupiettes de Sole and Les Poussins à la Rake garnis.'

Among Vincent O'Brien's many memorable successes, like his three successive Grand National winners, Early Mist, Royal Tan and Quare Times, must be ranked Ballymoss, who was ridden to victory in the Irish Derby in 1957 by T.P. Burns and who went on to capture the Prix de L'Arc de Triomphe on the day of Pope Pius XII's death the following year. The owner was John McShane, the American race sponsor, whose string included another famous winner, Gladness. Both of these horses were immortalised when McShane founded the Gladness Stakes and the Ballymoss Stakes which are still run annually at the Curragh.

McShane was a man of means. For years Bing Crosby's popular song had been posing the question; 'How can you buy Killarney?' In 1956 McShane furnished the reply by giving a sizeable sum to the trustees of the seventh Earl of Kenmare, who had put 8,300 acres of what is now the Killarney National Park, including two of the magnificent lakes and fells, on the market.

Staying at the Shelbourne McShane had become acquainted with Dennis McGeary who had been the manager since 1957. McGeary's efficient management style impressed the millionaire and the two became friendly in spite of the fact that McGeary, unlike his predecessor Barney Molloy, did not share McShane's interest in horses and racing. The American's property portfolio included the Berkeley Hotel in Philadelphia and he offered McGeary the job of managing it. The offer was accepted and McGeary left for the States in 1962.

His management position was taken over by Eoin Dillon who had previously worked at the Gresham. He was the brother of the novelist,

Eilis Dillon, whose best known work is *Across the Bitter Sea.* Barney Molloy, who was still looking after public relations, died that year. Eoin Dillon's first innovation as manager was a new restaurant, the Saddle Room, which became one of the most successful facilities ever in the history of the hotel. Former patrons still wonder, regretfully, why it ever closed.

It was sited in the former coffee room, the long room looking out on Kildare Street which is now the Shelbourne Bar. The access doors to the main dining room at the south end of the room were sealed and a handsome fireplace was installed. A fashionable false ceiling lowered the height of the room. When the Shelbourne Bar opened in 1991 this was removed and the original, elaborate cornice is now once again visible.

Eoin Dillon was aware that an equine theme still had a market appeal and the décor of the room was designed and executed accordingly. The final touch was to be an actual saddle, displayed close to the entrance. The manifold skills required to manage a large hotel do not normally include selecting horse trappings and the recently deceased Barney Molloy was probably the only member of the management team who could have been entrusted with the task. The budget for this acquisition was risibly small so it was hardly surprising that the piece of tack eventually acquired for the allotted fiver gave rise to cruel mirth amongst horsey diners. Fortunately it was placed so near the entrance that its inadequacies were quickly hidden beneath discarded coats at mealtimes.

The shameful saddle was finally retired from service through the charity of Sir John Galvin. Recognising that it struck a jarring note in a restaurant which was, in all other respects, superb, he donated a magnificent silver embellished Western saddle, in keeping with the quality of the surroundings. The silver trappings remained intact until Ronald Reagan visited Ireland. When the former cowboy actor admired the quality of the piece, some of the bullion was detached and presented to him as a souvenir.

As a restaurant the Saddle Room was a little to the right of middle market. It was crisp and civilised in the old tradition. A meal there cost about £6, as opposed to a little less than £3 in the adjacent Grill Bar, which had opened in 1959 in the rooms now occupied by the Side Door Restaurant.

The actor John Hurt, arriving in Dublin in 1964, remembers vividly how he fell in love with the Saddle Room on that first visit. He was starring in a Dublin Theatre Festival production of *Little Malcolm And His Struggle Against the Eunuchs* in the Gaiety Theatre. The festival was an exciting and internationally respected event. The budget of a stage production did not run to a bed in the Shelbourne but Hurt quickly discovered its other attractions. Like so many other artists who had worked in the Gaiety since it opened its doors in 1870 he was quick to recognise the convenience and comfort of the adjacent hotel. Now that he is resident in Ireland he is a familiar figure in the hotel's public rooms and, like many others, fondly remembers the Saddle Room as the jewel in the Shelbourne's crown. He loved the way that it could be 'tremendously elegant without being posh'. It had an easy going dignity which typified, for him, the spirit of the city. After the vastness of London he was captivated by the intimacy and diversity of a small town which managed to be, at the same time, a real capital city.

Even the sounds of Dublin had their own unique character. Horse-drawn drays still rumbled over cobbled streets and newspaper vendors hawked the 'Herald' or 'Press' in a nasal Dublin patois. In the Shelbourne liveried page boys, with gravity-defying pill box hats and impenetrable accents, went about summoning clients in a quaintly archaic sing-song. Hurt, who can still reproduce the sound perfectly, was unaware that their operatic delivery was the result of rigorous coaching by the head porter, who had himself learned the technique in his own paging days. The tradition of teaching the boys to sing announcements in a voice pitched well above the clatter of teacups went back a century to the opening of John McCurdy's new building. Guests accustomed to tannoy announcements elsewhere found the custom pleasantly nostalgic.

The late-night haunts available after a show came down were, in those days, fewer than at present. One of the most colourful was Peter Powrie's restaurant, The Soup Bowl, in Schoolhouse Lane, off Molesworth Street. Duck was the signature dish in the small, converted mews restaurant and almost every celebrity who visited the city sampled it. The other unforgettable after-hours spot for any working actor was the back room of Groome's Hotel, opposite the Gate Theatre. A seedy spot, of doubtful legality, it was always crammed with poets, politicians, journalists, actors and other insomniacs of Dublin's night-town. The ease with which these disparate elements mingled, drank and established a *lingua franca* astonished Hurt.

John Hurt (right) and the Hon. Garech Browne chatting outside the Shelbourne entrance, October 1999 (photo Sarah Owens).

Three years later, back in Dublin to star in John Huston's *Sinful Davy*, he became a Shelbourne resident. His sojourn reinforced his initial impressions of a great European hotel in the old tradition and many of the compatible friendships formed there then have endured. Compared to other capitals, Dublin was cheap. A return air fare to London cost less than £20 but for a foreign artist, unburdened by Joycean baggage, the cultural life here was the most accessible bargain of all. As an outsider he could relish it without having to mount constant guard against the native begrudgery syndrome, so well summed up by George Bernard Shaw:

> If you put an Irishman on a spit you will always find another Irishman to baste him.

Shortly after the release of *Sinful Davy* Hurt returned to play opposite Peter O'Toole in a Gaiety production of Shaw's *Man and Superman*.

Once again the Shelbourne was his base and the show was rehearsed in a private room on the first floor. He was impressed by the staff's tolerance of the foibles of residents. One evening, seated alone in the grandeur of the main dining room, he scanned the rarities of the menu with a jaded eye and confided to the waiter that, after weeks of *haute cuisine*, he could just fancy some common fish and chips in newspaper. The dish that was served was a triumph of gastronomic diplomacy. Between the fine bone china plate and the food there was an intervening rectangle of neatly clipped newspaper. Battered cod and chips were artistically aligned below the masthead of *The Irish Times.* His enduring memory of Dublin in those days is that it was deeply romantic.

CHAPTER NINE

HUNTING HAZARDS

... life goes on as it did elsewhere until 1939

Other changes were afoot in the Shelbourne in those early Trust House days. Although an electrically operated luggage lift had been installed in the late forties, guests were still transported in the beautiful but temperamental, hydraulic lift, which had plagued generations of operators. It was replaced by the existing installation in 1960. Vertical journeys throughout the six-storey building would no longer depend on the skill and judgment of lift attendants hauling on counterweighted ropes to transport their human cargo. Noel Sheehan, who had the job of doing this for many years has never forgotten how tricky it could be to keep control of an overloaded car, particularly on the downward journey. The rope, which was as thick as a ship's hawser, could slip off the cogwheels of the drive mechanism down in the basement and passengers were left stranded while the attendant hurried to the bowels of the building to try and re-engage the system. The open cage design of the old lift car had afforded an endless panorama of slowly gliding guests to anyone sitting on the mezzanine. With the introduction of an electrically operated closed lift car, entertainment gave way to efficiency.

The present Shelbourne garage was also purchased at that time from Neuman's Motors opposite the Kildare Street entrance of the hotel. There was some foresight in this acquisition since parking cars had not then become a problem in Dublin.

The character of the Shelbourne Rooms was due for modification too. The Horseshoe Bar had not only closed direct indoor access to the cocktail bar, it had also seduced a great many of the regular customers. Businessmen and serious trenchermen had been given a spiritual home in the Saddle Room, but the town had little to offer ladies who preferred to lunch lightly. In those pre-liberated days, wives of country squires and professional Mammons had a surfeit of leisure hours to fill. Shopping, fittings, hairdos and the manifold requirements of marriageable daughters filled whole days in town.

With their requirements in mind the foremost part of the Shelbourne Rooms was converted into The Causerie, a comfortable place to recuperate after fatiguing trawls through Brown Thomas and Switzers. It offered an unparalleled view of the passers-by in Stephen's Green and the open sandwiches from the smorgasbord could be lubricated by a discreet cocktail or two.

Although feistier women were starting to broach the traditionally male preserves of the pub, such women were still considered rather fast. One of the few haunts where a lady could drink without censure was in the enclosure at the races. An interest in the turf lent a certain legitimacy to propping up the bar. One well-known doyenne of the sport of kings, who had spent a hilarious day exploiting this privilege to the full, returned to the Shelbourne to order a taxi for the airport. While waiting for it she had a few more in the Horseshoe Bar and, by the time she set off to catch her plane to Paris, her enthusiastic consumption was taking its toll. Her own recollection of subsequent events was hazy but creative gossip soon filled the gaps. She remembered nothing about her journey until she woke, prone on a stretcher, in front of an altar blazing with candles. Organ music swelled on incense laden air and other stretcher cases were laid out around her on the ground like a fish kill.

Her condition on arrival at the airport had been so pitiable that she had been mistakenly assisted on to a plane carrying sick pilgrims to Lourdes. On arriving at the destination, still comatose, she had been carried to the Basilica with the other invalids. Her awakening brought about instant sobriety. As she staggered to her feet the congregation also rose in acclamation. In a sense they were right. Her resurrection might not have been a *bona fide* miracle but it was certainly a cure.

The hunting field generated as much mythology as the turf and as the century advanced, women began to figure more among the 'characters' who rode to hounds. The Shelbourne's most exalted hunting lady had been the Empress Elizabeth of Austria who later spoke of her days in Ireland as among the happiest in her life. She was one of the legendary beauties of her age and a fearless equestrienne. Her riding habits were cut like a second skin to enhance her slim figure and handspan waist. The garments made no concession to comfort but, in spite of this, she would lead the field all day, tireless and exhilarated. The flowing draperies of the side-saddle habit looked graceful on almost anyone but imposed restrictions. It was easier for women riders to compete and play a more prominent role in field sports when conventions allowed them the freedom of riding astride.

In the hunting hierarchy the most prestigious, demanding and costly role was that of Master of Foxhounds. Until the recent revulsion against blood sports, an MFH enjoyed considerable status in the community and repaid it by controlling pests and protecting livestock. Preserving and improving the working hounds is part of the job and nobody could be more committed to this task than Lord Daresbury, who with his wife and their close friend, Miss Merry Atkinson, was a constant visitor at the Shelbourne. Shortly after the war, Toby Daresbury became Master of the Limerick Hounds and immediately set about improving the quality of the pack. He acquired breeding stock from his friend the Duke of Beaufort who was Master of the Belvoir pack in Leicestershire and crossed them with native Limerick hounds. The result was an extraordinarily fine breed of foxhound, immortalised in many paintings by the Daresburys' close friend and hunting companion, Snaffles. Lord Daresbury's commitment to his pack endured until he died in his late eighties.

Two of his friends and fellow Masters who also figure prominently in the annals of the Shelbourne were, unusually for that time, women. One was Lady Cusack-Smith and the other became Melosine Bowes Daly after changing her name three times. She was born in 1910 near Athenry, County Galway. Her parents, Major and Mrs Cary Barnard led the typical Shelbourne patrons' life, with a comfortable home in the country and a base for urban entertainment in the hotel. It changed while Melosine was still very young. Her father was posted to the Dublin Garrison and, since security in the country had become precarious, the rest of the family followed him to town. They never returned to live in their house again. Although the property escaped burning it was looted and vandalised. Lloyds of London had withdrawn insurance cover from most of their Irish clients at that time and the Cary Barnards, like hosts of other displaced families, had to start life afresh.

Matters were not helped when Mrs Cary Barnard's throat was cut in an ambush. The wire, stretched across the road at the head height of a car passenger, had been intended for a British officer. It almost decapitated her and left her health permanently impaired. Like many other Anglo-Irish families they decided that the colonies might provide a preferable alternative to life in England and they re-located in East Africa for a period. Before they left, Melosine, at fourteen years of age, had laid the foundations of her future role as Master when she achieved the unique distinction of becoming the first girl ever to jump competitively in public. She was commended for completing two rounds at Badminton with only six faults. It was an impressive result for a young girl riding side-saddle in competition with seasoned cavalry officers.

When Major Cary Barnard died the East Africa chapter came to a close. Melosine had already eloped, at the age of seventeen, with a man twice her age and became, in due course, Mrs Trundle. The widowed Mrs Cary Barnard took up the threads of her former life and joined forces with another old Shelbourne connection, Alfred Chester Beatty. He gave her the job of managing his estate at Hartley Whitney. The Beattys had made their first visit to Ireland in 1937, registering at the Shelbourne on

30 August. They browsed the antique shops along the Quays and found the city agreeably old-world. It would seem even more so after World War II, which had precipitated difficult evacuations of Beatty's art treasures.

As 'New Britain' slid to the left, Ireland's conservatism offered an increasingly attractive quiet, non-bureaucratic location for the collection. In 1956 Beatty told the *Irish Tatler and Sketch*:

> Ireland is the best country in the world in which to retire. The country has atmosphere. The people have so much charm and life goes on as it did elsewhere until 1939.

The immediate post-war period was a time when many people felt unsettled. Melosine was one of them. The war had taken her to Bermuda, Egypt and the Low Countries and her marriage was over. She was staying with her mother and the Beattys at Hartley Whitney when, leafing through *Horse and Hound*, she saw that the Galway Blazers were looking for a Master. She wrote a letter offering her services and was astonished to get a positive response. Within days she was on her way to Dublin and the Shelbourne where she negotiated her appointment.

Initially, her industry and enthusiasm made her Mastership an unqualified success. Nobody in Galway seemed to care that she was divorced from her husband. Her marital status was tactfully ignored until she remarried. Her second husband, James Hanberry, was heir to one of England's stateliest homes, Birley House. Most people would have considered it a good match but the Irish hierarchy did not. Episcopal letters circulated through the diocese deploring the fact that the county had sunk low enough to honour a divorced woman with the Mastership of a pack of hounds and urging a boycott. Local allegiances were sharply divided on the matter. Some obeyed their pastors but others preferred to follow the hounds.

Hunt meets became highly dramatic. Melosine would bravely lead the hunt forth to draw the coverts, only to find non-hunting zealots barring the way with pitchforks. The clergy stirred the pot shamelessly and the situation deteriorated steadily. The new husband was minding his own business in England, probably unaware of the degree of hysteria that divorce and remarriage could provoke in Catholic Ireland. Melosine, determined to honour her obligations to the Hunt Committee, at least until the season ended, was beginning to wonder if her second marriage had been as big a mistake as her first. Whenever she could she escaped the controversy in Galway, making short journeys over to England via the Shelbourne.

Salvation came from an unexpected quarter when the Blazers' former Master, Dennis Bowes Daly reappeared on the scene. Although he was not initially sympathetic he was part of the familiar and comforting Shelbourne world of the Cary Barnards, Daresburys and Beattys in a way that the new English husband was not. For the second time in her life Melosine eloped, changing her name for the third and final time. After spending several years in East Africa the Bowes Dalys returned to Irish country life with their daughter, Denise. Shelbourne visits bracketed Denise's school terms like bookends. She remembers it as a place where, amidst the grandeur of the dining room, a homesick child could find plain rice pudding and compassion. Melosine Bowes Daly emigrated to Africa for the third time in 1996 and is now living in Durban with Denise.

Lady Cusack-Smith was another flamboyant figure of the hunting field. Born Molly O'Rourke, she hunted the Bermingham hounds in East Galway. She was the sort of sporting chatelaine who might have stepped straight from the pages of Somerville and Ross. Like Melosine Bowes Daly she was alarmingly competent, doing her own catering for her annual New Year's Ball in Bermingham House, Tuam and attending it in elegant ballgowns of her own design and manufacture.

Her table at the Horse Show Week balls in the Shelbourne was always lively. The unexpected often happened, sometimes disastrously, but her innate resilience always brought her bouncing back. She was a pragmatic woman. When travelling by train she was wont to order a treble pink gin in the buffet before departure because the delays in obtaining three separate shots might cause her to miss the train.

In one memorable conversation with Garech Browne she managed the considerable feat of emptying the Horseshoe Bar. It was early evening, before the influx of the regulars, and a discreet group of Americans were sipping cocktails. Years of hallooing across the hunting field had imparted a formidable timbre to Molly's voice. Sipping her gin and water she announced that she had been considering a face lift. She was particularly concerned about the vertical pleats which garnished her upper lip.

'It's because I blow so many horns,' she bellowed, 'As you know I have been at it since I was a slip of a girl.' The Americans began to look uneasy. Molly, oblivious, continued to pat the offending wrinkles. 'The one consolation is that all the men I know who blow horns have the wrinkles too and theirs are definitely worse than mine. Perhaps they put more effort into it'. The Horseshoe was suddenly deserted.

It was Lady Cusack-Smith who helped Brendan Behan to form his standard definition of a lady. In the summer of 1960 he attended a party in Jammet's restaurant, hosted by Lord Oranmore and Browne to celebrate the twenty-first birthday of his son, Garech. The fact that Behan was going through a rare period of sobriety sharpened his powers of observation. In the course of dinner he noticed Lady Cusack-Smith using her napkin as a handkerchief. 'A real lady', he said afterwards, 'is a woman who can blow her nose in her napkin and not worry about it'.

This entire equine confraternity swarmed into Dublin en masse for Horse Show Week. Normal life in the city was suspended and nowhere more than in the Shelbourne. Extra staff were hired, all leave was cancelled and nobody dared to even consider getting ill. Complex preparations were made in all departments of the hotel for the onslaught. The permanent valets on each floor had the busiest time of all. As a young porter, Noel Sheehan remembered how Paddy Bracken on the first floor, Bill Murray on the second, Paddy Kelly on the third, Tony McIvor on the fourth and Jim Casey on the fifth would face a whole week of sleepless nights, slaving over mountains of boots and saddles.

The gathering served more than one agenda for country families. The primary business and pleasure of the week revolved round the ubiquitous horse but the social round which could be lively to the point of mayhem, had an important subtext. Although career opportunities for girls were becoming broader, matrimony remained the most desirable option for many. Women's positions in the workplace were badly remunerated and insecure and women were discouraged from keeping their jobs after marrying. Many organisations, including state and semi-state agencies, operated a marriage bar, which made women ineligible for employment unless they remained single.

Given these conditions, a good match was the safest route to security and status. Times had not changed so much since George Moore wrote *A Drama in Muslin.* Daughters had to be settled as expeditiously as possible. The Horse Show teemed with the sort of eligible men who were scarcer than hens' teeth at any other time of the year. Whole regiments of them travelled over from England, furnishing an invaluable mating pool. When the fillies on sale in the Royal Dublin Society had two legs rather than four, the purchasers had to be carefully vetted too. Romance blossomed all too easily at the Horse Show and it behoved parents of débutantes to be wary. In the highly charged atmosphere of the RDS young women were highly susceptible.

A classic example of a disastrous misjudgment was the case of seventeen-year-old Bridget Dowling. In 1910 she attended the Horse Show with her father, who fell into conversation with a nattily dressed foreigner. The stranger was handsome and plausible. A heavy gold watch chain was stretched across his cream waistcoat and he sported two rings on his little finger, one set with a diamond, the other with a ruby. He introduced himself and a short conversation sufficed to establish that he was a wealthy Austrian hotelier, touring Europe to take a closer look at developments in the industry. Even his name, Alois Hitler, was exotic.

'Everything he said was so new and interesting that even his broken English seemed charming,' Bridget admitted ruefully, years later, 'Need I say that I was already head over heels in love?' She eloped. Her father was furious, having discovered by then that the handsome Alois was, in fact, a penurious commis waiter working in the Shelbourne Hotel. He wanted to have the abductor charged as a kidnapper. Sadly, for Bridget, Mrs Dowling intervened with more moderate advice and the couple were married in a hasty ceremony in London.

Bridget's life might have been easier if her father's counsels had prevailed. Alois was an improvident husband and an unsatisfactory father. He left his wife and child in 1914 to return to Germany and several years later they were told that he had died fighting in the Ukraine.

In fact he had bigamously remarried in Germany. That was bad enough but a greater embarrassment for the Dowling family would be Bridget's half-brother-in-law, Adolf, who was beginning to make something of a name for himself. In her memoirs Bridget wrote that Adolf stayed with herself and Alois in their Liverpool flat from November 1912 to April 1913 when he was trying to avoid being drafted into the Austrian army.

Many parents, wishing to avoid similar disasters for their daughters organised private receptions. The expense was a sound investment as a carefully monitored guest list reduced the risk of unsuitable liaisons for the girls. The problem was that, with so many parties in one week, festive appetites became jaded. As well as the show itself and the private parties, there were Bloodstock Sales in Goffs across the road from the showgrounds and racing in the evenings, in Phoenix Park. The greatest challenge for hosts was planning a party that would be remembered. In 1963 Captain and Mrs Jury, in the words of the *Daily Mail* society columnist, Charles Greville, 'carried off the title of the most ingenious hosts of the week.'

Master Chef, Maurice O'Looney.

Their private dance in the Shelbourne kitchens dominated every Irish and English gossip column. This was an impressive achievement in a week in which a sheep attended a diplomatic corps reception. The guest list glimmers like a lost galaxy and Maurice O'Looney, the Shelbourne's master chef for decades, presided over the meal and the construction of the ice sculptures created to enclose the candles. He had started life as a page boy and had gradually risen to preeminence as the establishment's master chef. The spaghetti and cannelloni which was served at this and subsequent kitchen suppers was the last word in early sixties cosmopolitan chic. The William Hickey column in the *Daily Express* described the evening:

> With nine hunt balls and innumerable private parties the Horse Show has now become a desperate quest for gimmicks.
>
> Mayfair mayhem is out this year and that leaves the hosts and hostesses of the almost exhausted debs and their escorts with a very real problem of what to put in its place.
>
> Of course if you own a big hotel the question is simplified. Captain Peter Jury who owns the Shelbourne Hotel put on a superb private party for upwards of 200 of his friends – in the kitchens.
>
> The guests filed past two huge barrels of wine presided over by a key bedecked cellarman to kitchens decorated with ice models of rabbits and swans.
>
> Captain Jury said: 'I thought it would be quite pleasant to have a private party for some of my friends during the hectic round of show week but it's terribly hard to find something new. Things seem to have quietened down considerably. I've suggested to the show committee that they should think seriously of organising evening bullfights …

Things would quieten down even more in the years to come. The tribal rites of the Horse Show were in their Indian Summer. John Hurt, encountering the rituals of the week for the first time in the late sixties was impressed by its 'serious elegance'. Formal clothing was a caste mark and people changed to dine out, even in the country where they had to brave long, freezing drives. Amenities like car heaters and de-misters were only available in the latest and most luxurious cars. In town, where travelling to a party was less of an ordeal, more extravagant style could be paraded. The Cotton Ball, organised by the Kildare Hunt on the Monday of Horse Show week, made some concessions to more casual attire but the dances organised by the Louth, the Galway Blazers, the Meath, the Ward Union and others were rigorously formal. The week's most pompous affair was the British Legion Ball, an annual fixture which Peter Jury, as a former officer, always secured for the Shelbourne ballroom.

A re-creation of a horse in the Shelbourne Ballroom.

It was an exhausting week for everyone involved. Head banqueting waiter Claude Spillane and his team served an endless series of dinners, late suppers and early breakfasts. The Galway Blazers always had a cooked breakfast at 4 a.m. which had to be professionally presented amidst the detritus of a night's hard drinking. Earl Gill still maintains that never again in his career did he encounter the raw vitality which characterised those hunt balls. Long days in the saddle seemed to imbue even the elderly with superhuman staying power. By the end of the week he and the band scarcely knew whose hunt ball was raging around them. On one such night, tired after a series of early morning finales, he slipped off to the bar for a quiet drink while supper was being served. A striking figure, attired in sequins and a blonde wig approached and asked huskily 'When do you want me?' Gill and the barman did a double-take before realising that this was Billy Quinn, the drag artist who had, apparently, been hired as a cabaret turn. A time was fixed for Quinn's entrance and Gill finished his drink and returned to the bandstand.

Had he been less tired he probably would have thought it was an eccentric choice of entertainment for that particular evening, which was not a rowdy hunt ball but the far stuffier British Legion affair. However Quinn's act was duly introduced and he kicked off the proceedings with a song entitled *Johnny's Little Yo-yo Isn't What It Used To Be.* An initial stunned silence was broken by apoplectic splutterings from purple faced colonels and majors. Ladies were hastily escorted from the room as Peter Jury hurried to the bandstand and hissed: 'What the hell is he doing here? Get him off.'

The indignant drag artist was railroaded out to the reception area with the organising committee of the British Legion in hot pursuit. Gill was summoned out to arbitrate in the argument. Quinn, sequins and eyes flashing and wig in hand was demanding his fee. The legionnaires were in unanimous agreement that, having been insulted by that sort of filth, they would certainly not pay the creature to go away. Quinn appealed to Gill. The committee, he insisted, had booked him months ago. Then, staring at the elderly military types around him he asked uncertainly: 'This is the Meath Hunt Ball isn't it?' He was despatched hastily by taxi to the Gresham where the Meath were holding their dance that year since their usual booking for the Shelbourne had been pre-empted by the British Legion.

The pattern of most hunt balls was so predictable that some English newspaper correspondents filed their copy hours before the dance started. Company Secretary, Paddy Shortall, whose career in the Shelbourne spanned forty-five years often heard a racy account of the night yet to come being filed from the hotel's public telephone booth. The photographs illustrating the column were also taken in advance. Journalists and debutantes alike preferred to get business out of the way before the real fun started.

A certain amount of rowdiness was expected at hunt balls. Wholesome, uncomplicated young people were meant to be high-spirited. Often food and drink were lobbed across the tables which is probably why some hunt ball suppers were kept simple. Culinary endeavour was wasted on comestibles that ended up as airborne missiles. The balconies of the Shelbourne ballroom offered excellent opportunities for this sort of well-heeled hooliganism. The real feast was one of misrule.

Nevertheless there was a definite etiquette encoded in the rituals. In spite of the hazards, dress codes were strictly observed at evening parties and daytime events made sartorial demands too. Women with an inelastic dress allowances could be hard pressed to equip themselves for the social calendar. Some, like Lady Cusack-Smith, put in painstaking hours of needlework or used the services of a local seamstress, but it was inconceivable not to make the effort.

Luckier socialites could choose their outfits from the collections of Irene Gilbert, Mary O'Donnell or Sybil Connolly. Later in the decade Clodagh O'Kennedy, Pat Crowley and Ib Jorgensen became the new desirable labels. Dublin couturiers at that time revived many Irish textiles as an international fashion medium. Donegal tweed, Irish poplin, pleated linen and Carrickmacross lace had become the signature fabrics of the day. Donald Davies of Enniskerry pioneered gossamer tweed with such success that by the time he opened his Paris boutique in 1968 he was exporting eighty-five per cent of his ready to wear garments.

A designer who made only unique original garments for her clients was Mrs Fitzsimons, who designed under her maiden name, Margaret Blythe, at 18 Kildare Street. The premises is now occupied by Cleo, a specialist design outlet for Irish tweeds and woollens, but in the sixties, Margaret Blythe's business was thriving there under the management of her sister, Florence Davenport. Her meticulous handiwork was particularly popular with the racing set who could call when they were ensconced over the road in the Shelbourne. Rita Hayworth commissioned many outfits when staying there and always brought her husband, Aly Khan, to fittings with her. Margaret Blythe had mixed feelings when she learned that some of her international clients were in the habit of attributing her designs to well-known Paris designers.

Escaping the bustle of the business for a quiet lunch or tea in the adjacent hotel was a daily occurrence for the designer and her talented daughters. Although none of them followed in her footsteps as designers they were all gifted. One of them, Margot, was an outstanding horsewoman who went on to enjoy considerable success as a breeder and competitive rider in America.

Another, Peg, was selected for training as a lyric soprano by Mother Clements when she was a pupil at the Dominican Convent in Eccles Street. Mother Clements had dedicated her life to fostering musical talent and had been Margaret Burke Sheridan's first teacher. Her plans for Peg's career were frustrated when Peg, her prize pupil, entered the convent. Mother Clements attacked the Mistress of Novices with entirely secular fury, exclaiming, 'How dare you take MY voice!

A third Fitzsimons sister, Maureen, studied acting a few doors away from the family business in the Mary Burke Elocution School, next door to Mitchell and Sons Wine Merchants. In 1937 she won the Dawn Beauty contest in Dublin, starting a career which would lead to Hollywood, a change of name to Maureen O'Hara and fifty-odd feature films.

Maureen's lifelong association with the Shelbourne had made it as familiar and comfortable as a second home. On a visit home from Hollywood, unable to do full justice to a delicious dinner, she asked for a doggy bag. The staff who had known her since childhood complied cheerfully but her Aunt Florence was mortified. Much later she learned that she had been the first person ever to ask for a doggy bag in the Shelbourne dining room.

Her happiest memories of the hotel are of visits shared with her husband, General Charles Blair. General Blair was the most distinguished aviator of his generation, holding an impressive number of flying records, many of which have never been equalled. He made the first jet fighter flight over the North Pole and his 1951 record for trans-Atlantic crossing by piston-engined plane still stands. In 1944 he flew the five fastest seaplane crossings from America to Ireland on consecutive trips, using the Foynes harbour terminal. General Blair's career brought him frequently to Ireland. He landed the first seaplane at Foynes and flew the last one out, after which he piloted the first trans-Atlantic flight to Rineanna, later to be renamed Shannon.

The Blairs often used the Shelbourne on family visits to Dublin. As far as the General was concerned the place had only one shortcoming. Like many other European hotels it had no exercise facilities. At his home, in the Virgin Islands, Charles Blair followed a regular fitness routine but he soon realised that there would be a problem maintaining it in Dublin, where voluntary exertion was still considered peculiar.

Hall porter, Noel Sheehan had his first brush with this alien concept when an American lady checked into room 504. Americans were generous tippers in those days and Jim, the porter who attended her to her room returned to base at the front desk, mildly disappointed that he had received no gratuity. Shortly afterwards the new arrival telephoned the desk to enquire if there was a gym in the hotel. Noel, thinking that she was intending to rectify her recent oversight, replied helpfully that the hotel actually had three of them, namely Jim Cochrane, Jimmy Dixon and Jim O'Keefe, whom she had just met when he carried her bags upstairs. There was a long pause before she mystified him by asking: 'Do they teach aerobics?'

Charles Blair was more realistic. As a seasoned world traveller he could grasp the practical limitations. He worked out his own solution. Each morning he arrived down in the lobby, impeccably groomed and tailored for a day in the city. There was always a folded mackintosh over his arm and if the weather was wet he would put it on over his suit. He was an impressive, military figure, six foot three inches tall, athletic and handsome. After exchanging a few remarks with the staff on duty he strolled through the revolving door and along the Green. As soon as he was out of sight of the hotel he began to run. His speed could never be mistaken for jogging as he pounded through the streets in beautifully polished shoes, the mackintosh flapping over his arm. His route circled the perimeter of the Green and covered the length of Grafton Street, Nassau Street and Merrion Square, dodging pedestrians and taking lethal risks with traffic. Approaching the hotel again he would straighten his tie, adjust the folds of his mackintosh and saunter back into the lobby. The staff at the front desk never understood why the General's wife was so relieved to see him returning from his daily constitutional in one piece.

CHAPTER TEN

VALE CAPTAIN JURY

between the patrician past and the egalitarian future…

In the summer of 1968 trouble flared in Northern Ireland, starting an unremitting cycle of bombs, barricades, reprisal and counter-reprisal. In the same year, a statue of Robert Emmet was unveiled in St Stephen's Green but the time had obviously not yet come for his long overdue epitaph. The first death in the cycle of violence occurred the following July of 1969, when a seventy-year old farmer was killed in a faction fight outside the Dungiven Orange Hall in County Derry.

The whole country took several steps backwards both economically and ecumenically. Inevitably, Ireland's appeal as a tourist destination was tarnished by the violence. British business, which was then our most significant source of tourist revenue declined dramatically. No hotelier was happy about the situation but Peter Jury had more worries than most.

The Shelbourne had survived lean times in the past but then policy decisions had rested solely in the hands of the Cotton Jury clan.

Now management decisions required the approval of a geographically remote head office. Initially, the Trust Houses deal seems not to have impinged too much on Peter Jury's autonomy but corporate culture was in a state of flux. It was not an easy time to lose control of a family business.

The dawn of the seventies saw endings as well as beginnings. The wonder horse, Arkle was put down and the 'King of the Pipers', Leo Rowsome, died in September. For a while that year it seemed that the traditional music renaissance was threatened. In March, Seán Ó Ríada's classical work, *Hercules Dux Ferrariae* was published, both as a manuscript and a recording. The official launch of the work was held in the Hibernian Hotel and the signing of the scores took place in the Shelbourne, where he was staying.

At the same time, he made an unexpected announcement in a radio interview that he intended to disband Ceoltóirí Cualainn, the folk orchestra which had been launched in the Shelbourne ballroom. After the announcement Paddy Moloney of the Chieftains rang Ó Ríada at the Shelbourne, and begged him to reconsider but the composer's health was failing and he remained adamant about his decision. The coolness between the two was resolved before Ó Ríada's death the following year. John Montague recalls a party in Garech Browne's house, Woodtown Manor. As Moloney concluded a piece on the tin whistle Ó Ríada clapped him on the back and called him 'the best musicianer in Ireland'. Montague insists that the word 'musicianer' was crucial because it implied the all-round ability of 'the man with the music.' It seemed, he said, 'that Seán was passing on the reins to Paddy.'

Other differences that arose at that time were harder to resolve. A leaner, meaner spirit of enterprise was in the air. For Peter Jury, amusing interludes like private parties in the hotel kitchens had been succeeded by seismic upheavals in the London head office. Large companies, possibly because they still had some vestigial distaste for doing their own hatchet jobs, were depending increasingly on impartial management consultants to restructure their organisations. The bottom line for consultancy firms was profitability. They had little sympathy for the softer aspects of corporate culture. Trust Houses had retained McKinseys, one of the most prestigious international firms. Their recommendations sowed the seeds of discord between the board of Trust Houses (Ireland) and the

London office. In 1968 a memorandum to Peter Jury recapitulated the McKinsey recommendations which had caused concern in Ireland:

> Prior to May 1968, Trust Houses (Ireland) operated as an autonomous company within the Trust Houses Group and, following the principles that were established in other parts of the group, the Managing Director reported to his own board and only indirectly to the central executive of the Group. The local Board was responsible for the finances of the Company, the profitability and well being of the Company.

This, according to McKinseys, had to change. Their report had highlighted the dangers of fragmentation 'and the detrimental effect that it had on the profitability of the Group';

> They set down as a major pre-requisite of a successful operation that the senior executive responsible for any section of the Group should be personally responsible for the profitability of that section and that no Board or Committee, apart from the parent Board of the Group, should hold profit responsibility.

All the United Kingdom boards had already been put into cold storage. Although the Irish board would continue to function, it would operate differently, with tight budgeting, central control and yardsticks of management efficiency as the ominous improvements on former arrangements.

> It is clear, with the advantages of hindsight, that these principles were not adequately explained to yourself or to members of the Board of Trust Houses (Ireland). In applying them to Ireland it is important that we arrange the relationship in a way that takes account of the individuality of Ireland (the same applies to other overseas operations) but at the same time allows maximum use of the central staff know how and a rapid and clearly defined decision-making line for yourself as Managing Director.

Jury was to report thenceforth to the author of the memorandum, Michael Pickard, and would be personally responsible for the profitability of the Irish group. It was suggested that monthly management meetings of the Irish board should cease and be replaced by quarterly discussions. Jury himself would be invited to attend a central board meeting each quarter although:

> Again this is not a decision-making occasion but an opportunity to exchange information. I am aware that because of shortcomings at this end Trust Houses (Ireland) Ltd has had some problems in its dealings with central departments. It is hoped that in future these relationships will work more smoothly.

It seemed unlikely that this would be the case given the sugar-coated pill that followed. Peter Jury had, up to then, had control of project management in Ireland. Now any project costing in excess of £40,000 would be subject to the decisions of a central development committee and a technical services department based in London. It must have been poor consolation to Peter Jury to be assured that, under this arrangement he would not have to concern himself about too many problems. The Irish board members were greatly valued, the document concludes, but it is difficult to understand quite why since:

> We do not believe that non-executive members of a Board can make a real contribution to the day to day running of any hotel operation.

The last of the Cotton Jurys was in his fiftieth year. Only two years previously, in January 1967, a Grand Centenary Ball had been organised by Eoin Dillon to mark the centenary of Messrs Cotton, Jury and Goodman's establishment. It had been a lavish celebration of continuity and tradition.

Peter Jury's opening remarks underscored his changed status in his family's former fiefdom:

> Ladies and Gentlemen, I am here to represent the present proprietors of the Shelbourne Hotel, although,

> as you will have realised as you filed in we have the pleasure of having nearer relatives than I am, of the present owners with us tonight in the persons of two Executive Directors of Trust Houses.
>
> To-night's party marks the 100th Anniversary of the re-opening of the Shelbourne in its present form – give or take a little – by my forebears of three generations back.

He went on to pay tribute to Martin Burke as a man of 'some National Significance'. His recapitulation of the Shelbourne's history is brief but nostalgic and ends with the injunction:

> Begone dull care – make room for mirth and glee.

Unfortunately the new owners' zeal for change and reform would make it difficult for Jury himself to realise that aspiration in coming years. Finding himself deprived of the active support of his Irish board and cast in the role of David opposite the Trust Houses' Goliath he must have felt dangerously exposed.

In the year of the hotel's centenary Sally and Peter Jury and their young daughters Sophie and Polly had moved from Killiney to Struan Hill, Enniskerry. The family saw in the New Year of 1969 without their father. He had gone to London to see Lord Crowther, the Trust Houses Chairman but the meeting was aborted. Lord Crowther, replying on 2 January to an earlier letter from Sir George Mahon, a member of the Irish board, wrote:

> Unfortunately I was laid up yesterday and did not see Peter.

He goes on to protest:

> I want to say as emphatically as I can that there is no question whatever of the Irish Directors outstaying either their welcome or their usefulness. Quite on the contrary. We greatly and sincerely value their counsel and help and would be distressed if we were deprived of them.

I cannot help thinking that – doubtless through faults of communication on my part – the changes that are contemplated have assumed, in Peter's mind and in yours, a dimension far greater than they deserve. In particular I wish to remove the impression there is any 'injustice to Ireland' involved.

It is clear, with the advantages of hindsight, that you have not been adequately informed on the policies of Trust Houses. I think I have been waiting for questions which possibly you did not think it appropriate to ask. In any case, for the future, let there be a policy of full disclosure.

At the same time, we suggest that the Board should no longer concern itself with details of management, for which the Managing Director should be personally responsible, reporting directly to the Group Managing Director in London. It is therefore suggested that the monthly meetings of the Executive Committee should lapse. We see this as an increase in Peter's personal responsibilities, and if it appears to be a reduction in the activities of the Board, it is surely a recognition of the fact that no Board can really be effective in matters of management …

We certainly do not intend 'Too tight control from U.K.' On the contrary the Managing Director will have complete freedom of action within his budget. He will, it is true, be expected to avail himself of the services of our specialist departments. The sore point, I know, is that Peter feels that the control of project management is to be taken out of his hands. This may or may not be the best way of doing things but it is obviously not an unreasonable way and we have no doubt at all that it is the most economical way.

A little later Crowther sent a brief note to Jury:

Would you drop me a line to say whether you are happy with the definition of functions that Michael (Pickard) showed you. I am conscious of the fact that failures of communication on my part have been largely

> responsible for raising apprehensions in your mind, which I honestly believe to be unjustified.

Later developments would more than justify Jury's apprehensions. The mandibles of corporate revision were gaping before him like Jonah's whale.

Several days later he drafted a reply to Crowther:

> Michael [Pickard] showed me the draft of the memorandum which I have since received. This seems to provide a better basis for me to operate than has been the case over the last six or eight months. I am making the assumption that in any diagrammatic layout of the group's 'establishment', Trust Houses (Ireland) will be at least equal to if not senior to Westminster, etc.
>
> As regards development which is rightly stressed as being a main point, on which I have had difficulty in adjusting any ideas, there would seem to be one major point of rationalisation remaining. It would be true to say that the Board of TH (I) does not have many functions left to it, if it does not have the chance of arguing through a case for some project or other across the table within its own ranks. Assuming that a fuller representative board is present on the occasion concerned. My understanding is that whatever conclusions were come to on such an occasion in the end result it would be a question of me fighting it out with the development committee. I must admit to finding such a procedure in danger of leading to frustration.
>
> I have not had an opportunity of talking to the Irish directors and therefore do not know their reaction.

The problems of managing the wholly owned subsidiary of a mammoth organisation were not ameliorated by Trust Houses' merger with the Forte Group in 1970. Forte, although the smaller organisation, immediately demonstrated superior political skill in seizing control of the newly merged group. Meanwhile, back in Ireland other practical problems bedevilled the hotel business when the banks went out on strike for six months. The financial chaos that this caused for businesses is hard to imagine today. Hotels, which of their nature dealt with transient custom, were exposed to grave difficulties. The country ran on virtual finance and real worry.

Assessing the creditworthiness of clients had not become noticeably easier since the days of Barney Molloy. Padraic Browne who became general manager in 1968 had to spend a lot of time keeping one jump ahead of the chancers. On one occasion Browne received a telephone call from someone purporting to be Vincent O'Brien, asking him as a personal favour to cash a large cheque for a bloodstock agent travelling through Dublin. The voice and the references seemed right and Browne agreed but then began to wonder if the request was not quite O'Brien's style. He called the O'Brien household and was told that O'Brien had not made the call and was unacquainted with the bloodstock agent

Pre-empting a sting could misfire sometimes. Credit cards were an exotic rarity and cheques were not underwritten by guarantees so there was no way of collecting a deposit from last minute telephone bookings. Previously unknown individuals arriving by taxi late at night on foot of a telephone call were potential embarrassments. One such late night arrival checked into a single room and instructed that a bottle of Dom Perignon should be served immediately and charged to his bill.

Early the following morning, Browne received a message from Room Service. The gentleman had ordered another bottle of Dom to be delivered to his room with a copious breakfast and a pitcher of fresh orange juice. It was fairly conspicuous consumption for a telephone booking but it might be impolitic to refuse service. Browne told them to go ahead with the order and leave him to contact the gentleman later about methods of payment. Ten minutes later an agitated waiter called to report that the single bed was now occupied by two champagne quaffing gentlemen.

It was an unusual enough situation in those days and one that definitely should be checked out before any more Dom was abstracted from the cellar. Browne rang and asked if he could come up and have a word. Within seconds of entering the room he was confident that the bill would be paid. The couple in the single bed could never have been aware of the speed with which their worth was assessed. While accepting their offer of a glass of champagne Browne had made a lightning inventory of the

Jermyn Street shirts and Saville Row tailoring spilling out of the Vuitton luggage. The dressing table was littered with male accessories by Gucci, Aspreys and Rolex. It was obvious that these people had been weaned on champagne and could afford any amount of it. The difficulty now was for Browne to explain his intrusive presence at the foot of the lovers' bed.

He sipped his champagne and orange juice thinking hard. When he rose to go he was asked what exactly he had wanted to discuss. It was a question that he still could not answer himself, so he explained that it had always been Shelbourne policy for the general manager to pay his respects personally to anyone stylish enough to order Dom Perignon for breakfast. He escaped down the corridor, feeling that his collar was suddenly a size smaller and reflecting that his morning had given a new meaning to the chapter of Elizabeth Bowen's memoir entitled *Gay Days.*

Even without a bank strike there was a necessity for constant vigilance about debts but with the financial institutions of the country on unofficial leave, cash management became a nightmare.

Cheque books were quickly exhausted and after that promissory notes were scribbled on any scrap of paper that came to hand. It was a fraudster's paradise. As the months went by even the most virtuous were tempted to award themselves an unapproved overdraft. Trade in portable goods boomed. New cars could be acquired and driven straight out of the country, leaving the dealer with a piece of paper that would never be redeemed. Businesses were faced with the choice of piling up wads of funny money or ceasing trade. Many of the ersatz cheques were endorsed and re-circulated several times over as cash was hard to access.

The return of the striking bank clerks caused even more anxiety than their long absence. The hoarded DIY cheques which flooded into the bank totalled an estimated seven to eight million pounds. Many of them were not honoured and no quarter was given to account holders forced into the red by the death, disappearance or deviancy of debtors. Businesses were forced into closure and others were left managing crippling debts.

Some Dublin hotels, even the most exclusive, had fared disastrously. Horror stories circulated and Padraic Browne could hardly believe, when the day of reckoning came, that the Shelbourne had come off so lightly.

Their worthless chits amounted to a fraction of those held by other establishments. The Shelbourne patrons might have been more ethical than others but it is, perhaps, more likely that they were reluctant to be barred from such an agreeable watering hole.

Meanwhile, over in London the power politics in Trust House Forte gathered pace oblivious. Differences among the old guard went into temporary abeyance as they closed ranks against the common enemy. In New Year 1972, Lord Crowther circulated a strictly confidential document to his old friends and colleagues in Trust Houses. The honeymoon with Forte was over and one of the casualties had been Michael Pickard, who had been instrumental in reducing the autonomy of Peter Jury – a cogent reminder that what goes around comes around. A bid from Allied Breweries was on the table:

> We have decided to recommend all the shareholders to accept the Allied bid, and we propose to do so for our own holdings. We have not reached this decision lightly and I would like to explain the arguments that have influenced us. They really fall under two heads – the dangers of leaving THF as it is, and the prospects of a better future with Allied …
>
> You all know, and I think share, the pride that I feel in Trust Houses as it now is – or at least as it was until recently.
>
> This is not the occasion to try to explain why we entered into the merger with Forte – I will only say that we did it in complete good faith and with high hopes. Nor is it the time to relate what went wrong with the merger – I think you all know or can guess, at least, some of the reasons. The fact is that, starting with the abrupt dismissal of Mr Pickard in July the Forte directors have succeeded in taking control of the management of the whole company. This is not at all what was agreed in 1970 but it is what has happened.
>
> If this were simply the substitution of one set of individuals for another, perhaps there would be no occasion for worry. But the fact is that, as we have learned over the past year, the Forte directors have very

> different ideas about running hotels from those that have always prevailed in Trust Houses. Mr Brian Franks has already resigned, and though ill health unfortunately played a part in his decision, the immediate occasion was a deep disagreement with Sir Charles Forte about maintenance policy. Mr Mathew's position is being made increasingly difficult. Other senior executives have already resigned and I know that others are determined to do so if Sir Charles Forte remains in control.
>
> There will be the severest pressure to make every possible penny out of the hotels in the short run you all know at what cost.

He then dealt with the knotty question of whether Trust Houses should come under the control of a brewer. Some years previously such an association would have been unthinkable but now it is more acceptable and, he asserts with touching faith:

> Trust Houses would continue as an autonomous entity, with its present name and, for all practical purposes, its present organisation.

Lord Crowther, as he stated with palpable relief in his closing paragraph, was close to retirement at that stage. He did not live long enough to enjoy it as he suffered a fatal collapse at an airport shortly afterwards. For Peter Jury the problems continued. The tourist trade was still in the doldrums. During 1971 the trouble in the North had escalated to the point where it threatened to spill across the border into the Republic. The year opened with a car bomb fatality in Sackville Place in Dublin. In February the British Embassy in Merrion Square, which had already been attacked several times by fire bombs, was burned out in the largest and most acrimonious demonstration that the city had ever witnessed. During that day the Shelbourne, as a British-owned concern, received several telephoned threats of violent reprisal.

The Welsh rugby team immediately cancelled their international fixture, scheduled for the following month at Lansdowne Road, as a result of the threats. This left the Shelbourne as deserted as the *Mary Celeste* for that weekend. The hotel was usually booked out for international rugby matches a year ahead. The Irish team and every visiting international team had always stayed there with the sole exception of the French, who preferred to plan their tactics in strategic isolation and eschewed mixing with the opposition until the post-match celebrations started. The fact that the teams were in residence naturally attracted droves of supporters. Ever since the 1950s, when players like Tony O'Reilly and the legendary fly-half, Jack Kyle, became the pop stars of their generation, the Shelbourne had been synonymous with international rugby. Any cancellation would reflect immediately in the accounts of the hotel.

It was a relief when the English team went ahead with their match as planned. When they emerged on to the pitch at Lansdowne Road they received a spontaneous standing ovation of two minutes duration. The boisterous, exhausting and profitable normality of a Rugby International weekend vibrated through the Shelbourne once again.

In November that year there was a bomb in the Irish Film Centre and the following month two more bombs in the city caused two deaths. Incendiary devices, bomb scares and hoax warnings were rampant. Day after day the city's thoroughfares were crowded with evacuees from the office blocks where bomb disposal teams were searching the interior.

British tourist receipts continued to drop like a stone. A memo, sent to Michael Jones in preparation for the November board meeting of 1972, confirmed the fact. Amongst the sales and marketing issues to be considered there is mention of a marketing franchise, designed to promote both Trust House Forte establishments and several independent hotels in Ireland as tourist destinations. The London office had never been quite at ease with the foreignness of their Irish region. After stressing the high degree of tourist emphasis in the country the memo stated:

> The collapse of the British market in particular has adversely affected this operation and currently it is of little value.

In spite of the recession in tourism and the power struggle behind the scenes, business proceeded as usual in the Shelbourne. Guests never ceased to make bizarre demands. When Peter O'Toole was back in Dublin in the early seventies performing in *Waiting for Godot* at the

Abbey Theatre he was unhappy about his make-up. No stage preparation, in his opinion, could reproduce the requisite scruffiness for Beckett's tramps. Acting upon O'Toole's instructions the stage manager called the front desk of the Shelbourne to request the immediate delivery of a bucket of soot. Noel Sheehan was despatched to the boiler room to fetch it. It would have been out of the question for him to return to his duties on the front desk looking like a chimney sweep but he managed, somehow, to extract the required amount of carbon from the boiler flues without getting a single speck on his uniform. The same resident made demands at the other end of the hygiene spectrum when he took the most extravagant bubble bath ordered in the Shelbourne to date. The members of staff detailed to fill it stoically concealed any regrets they might have felt as they emptied twenty-four magnums of the finest champagne into the star's bathtub.

In 1972, the Shelbourne made its final acquisition of property in St Stephen's Green when it bought the house and garden at number 34 from the Girl's Friendly Society. The façade now extended all the way from Kildare Street to the north west corner of the Green. The ground floor of the new acquisition was put to various uses over the years, housing the Paddock Bar and the Garden Suite of conference rooms. It is now the hotel's Health and Fitness Centre. An eighteen-metre swimming pool has been constructed on the site of the former garden. One of the more celebrated features of number 34 is a mural attributed to Angelica Kauffman.

Meanwhile Jury was still striving to safeguard his position within the Trust House Forte organisation. By October 1972 he believed that he had come to an agreement. Two weeks later it was obvious that he had not. The letter which he wrote to George Hendrie in London pointed out acerbically that they now seemed incapable of mutual understanding on the telephone. The sequence of events which he recapitulated was frustrating;

> I came to London on October 2nd to be present at the examination by Sir Charles Forte of the Irish budget for 1973. You arranged for me to lunch with you and Mr. Leach and the purpose of this was to tell me that a decision had been reached ... It would no longer be

> feasible for you to attend to Ireland as a separate unit and that the situation would revert to what it had been when Mr. Mathews was Managing Director of TH hotels and I ceased to report direct to Mr. Pickard. I informed you that would be unacceptable to me. You suggested I should give my reactions to this decision to Sir Charles.

Sir Charles Forte had calmed the situation by explaining that the situation outlined was nothing to worry about, merely 'different names on different doors' and assured Jury that he was still regarded as the Group's man in Ireland. Sir Charles had also expressed concern about Jury's conviction that the proposals had been framed with the intention of forcing his resignation.

After another trip to London a week later Jury was confident that he had worked out a tolerable deal whereby he would become Executive Chairman of the Irish board. Another week passed before Michael Jones arrived from head office with a radically different proposal, prompting the long, indignant letter to Hendrie. It met with a discouraging response. A non-executive chairmanship of indeterminate duration was the only sweetener offered with an effective dismissal; 'it is obvious that there has been a serious misunderstanding', Hendrie wrote:

> 'We had never contemplated that more than one person should be responsible for operating the Irish hotels and, as you declined to continue to discharge that responsibility under Mr. Leach, we agreed to transfer the responsibility to Mr. Jones.

The election of Michael Jones as managing director and Peter Jury as chairman was scheduled for the November board meeting. Once that procedure had been outlined Hendrie cut to the chase:

> for at least the next twelve months your salary should remain at its present level and the Company continue to pay your pension contributions and the contributions to BUPA. As chairman you will not be called upon to undertake any day to day duties therefore I am assuming

> you will no longer have any need for a permanent office. I have instructed Mr. Jones to see that office and secretarial facilities are available for you whenever you have any business to transact on behalf of the Company.
>
> At the end of a period of twelve months we both hope that you will have been able to involve yourself in other interests – in the light of the situation at that time we should then take the opportunity of revising your salary to a level more appropriate to your position as non-executive Chairman of the Board.

The puppeteer in London, who manipulated the strings of the Irish operation, was not aware that the British BUPA health scheme was unavailable in Ireland. Jury's situation was precarious and he had a young family to look after. Then, as now, redundancy could be disastrous for a man in his fifties. His colleagues, according to some notes scribbled at the Airport Hotel in Dublin, had advised him 'not to throw in the sponge yet' and he persisted in his efforts. By the end of October, he seemed to have bought a little time. He framed minutes of a meeting which had taken place with George Hendrie on 26 October:

> While not necessarily agreeing with all that I had said you confirmed the following as being acceptable.

It was a clear case of accepting half a loaf rather than no bread. Jury had asked to retain his company car and the part-time services of a secretary for a period of six months. He would be allowed an office, but this, too, was hedged around with conditions. He could only use it for company business and for the rest of the time it would be at the disposal of Michael Jones, the company's representative from London, and others at Mr Jones' discretion, The arrangement was to be reviewed after six months. It is hard to believe that the man who had, twelve years earlier, been described by Crowther as the best asset that the company had acquired in Ireland was reduced to framing Clause D:

> That I was free to draft a short contract for your consideration, which gave me greater assurance of continued remuneration than is contained in your letter

> of October 20th. You suggested that such a contract would be unlikely to be acceptable if it envisaged a period of more than 3 or 4 years.

The final three clauses were a last ditch attempt to salvage his health insurance, his pension scheme and some, albeit diminished, executive role in the company.

In fact the pension issue was never satisfactorily resolved. The Jury family, while exacting loyal service from employees, had always been scrupulous about making proper provisions for their retirement. It is ironic that the last family member working in the hotel should also be one of the first managers whose services to the Shelbourne were not fittingly rewarded.

By the middle of 1973 inflation was causing problems in Ireland and wage increases were running at twenty per cent. A further dramatic deterioration in the economy was precipitated by the OPEC oil crisis which followed the Arab–Israeli war of October. The entire western world was affected but Ireland, importing over seventy per cent of its primary energy requirements, was particularly vulnerable. Justin Keating likened the effect on the economy to 'falling off a cliff'. Recent election promises of reduced levies and increased welfare payments had to be honoured even though the cost of living had been sent soaring by a tenfold increase in oil prices.

Inevitably belt-tightening ensued and local usage of the Shelbourne slackened. Some hotel and leisure facilities closed their doors forever at that time and others reduced staff numbers considerably. The Shelbourne remained one of the more secure places for employees. Even with the falling numbers of guests the shortages made provision of hot water and laundry services extremely difficult. The tariffs had been set for a year ahead and the soaring cost of inputs generated by the fuel crisis squeezed margins to the bone.

Worse was to come with the introduction of the ill-conceived Wealth Tax. Despite its timing, the tax was not devised as a corrective measure for the miseries of the oil crisis. Garret FitzGerald had conceived the idea as far back as 1965 and it had been revived again in the 1973 election manifesto. The idea of an annual tax on assets created widespread consternation amongst the propertied classes. For those landed gentry who saw themselves as survivors of earlier anti-Ascendancy pogroms it threatened a further erosion of security. Rumours ran riot and it was feared that an arbitrary bureaucratic valuation might be placed on pictures, furniture and other heirlooms and that tax would be levied accordingly.

Taxing non-income earning assets on an ongoing annual basis was seen as tantamount to confiscation. The promise that death duties would be alleviated was inadequate compensation when some members of the Cabinet were proposing a rate as high as two-and-a-half or three per cent. In fact the tax, when it was finally enacted in 1975, was set at one per cent on all sums over £100,000 in 1974 terms but the damage was done. The exodus of wealth had started as soon as the tax was mooted. It is an article of faith that new taxes, once introduced, can only grow larger. Taxing assets was clearly the thin end of the wedge. People with independent means voted with their feet. The Isle of Man became log-jammed with the former chatelaines of Irish estates and many headed for sunnier climates in Europe or South Africa. The property pages of *Country Life* were crammed with Irish mansions and demesnes many of which went at bargain basement prices to foreigners and syndicates.

The revenue which the tax generated was hardly worth all the bother; a mere £3.5 million in 1975, rising to over £5 million in 1977. Commensurate losses on death duties were far higher and by the time the tax was scrapped in 1978 the damage was done.

Communising wealth was a less popular notion than had been anticipated in a country where many more people had started to entertain material aspirations. An atavistic distaste for the underlying principles of taxation led even those who would not be affected by the new levy to call Ritchie Ryan, the Minister for Finance 'Red Ritchie' and 'Ritchie Ruin'.

The numbers of old Shelbourne regulars were decimated. Padraic Browne who was managing the hotel at the time recalls that there was an instant 20 per cent drop in business. The tax caused a far greater setback in the hotel's business than either the fuel crisis or the political troubles. When the tax eventually proved to be counter-productive it was too late to help those businesses that had been damaged by the sudden disappearance of their most affluent clients.

The tax had certain limited uses. People's degree of panic about it could be a cogent indicator of their true worth. One ambitious mother used it as an infallible litmus test for potential sons-in-law. Hosting Shelbourne dinner parties for her marriageable girls she would defer her final placement until everyone had assembled for a pre-dinner sherry. As she pressed the hand of each bachelor arrival she murmured, her face furrowed with sympathy: 'My dear, will the wealth tax affect you awfully?'

Having checked out the eligibility of the assembled talent she would slip into the dining room with her place cards. Her daughters were sandwiched between the men who had responded to her question with a whole Christie's catalogue of potential tax burdens. Anyone who admitted that it would not affect them in the slightest was consigned to the far end of the table and never asked again.

Visible badges of prosperity had become more subtle. The bogeymen from the oil emirates and the tax inspector's office had made it less fashionable to flaunt wealth. The fuel crisis had created an awareness of diminishing resources. Vehicles, particularly, were being scaled down. Peter Jury wanted to exchange his company car for a smaller model. In his case there would seem to have been practical as well as ideological considerations governing the decision. Even in this modest objective, which would seem laudable in the light of the times, he encountered difficulties in his negotiations with head office.

The company car, a Rover 3.5 litre saloon, which he had been hoping 'to retain on the same basis as heretofore' the previous October had become a bone of contention by June 1973. The automatic transmission was defective and Jury had requested permission to exchange it for a 1.5 litre vehicle which would have had less than half of the engine capacity of the Rover and be cheaper to run. He was informed that the smaller car was not specified in the list which the Chief Executive had deemed suitable for issue to company employees.

George Hendrie's solution was to offer to sell the Rover to Jury at a privileged price of £1,133, after which he could exchange it for a privately-owned car of his choice. The problem was that the substitute, whatever it was, would no longer be a company car and the associated costs of upkeep would have to be borne by Jury personally. An offer of mileage for any trips made on company business was hardly a compensation as the Jury's active involvement in the company was obviously being eroded week by week. Insult was added to injury when Crawford's Garage placed a resale value of £1,150 maximum on the Rover but this was only conditional on the automatic transmission being repaired at Jury's own expense. This would cost £250. Jury fulminated to Hendrie:

> I don't need to tell you that the arithmetic involved in this makes your proposal of June 11th a very unattractive one for me.

An essentially trivial issue had been made into yet another bureaupsychotic nightmare. Verbal assurances from head office were negated by subsequent correspondence. Jury's background and army training meant that he kept a stiff upper lip throughout all his frustrations. Many of his letters were written by hand rather than typed in his office and even staff who worked closely with him had little notion of the extent of his problems.

Effectively the record of his active involvement with the Shelbourne ends with the wrangle over the company car. He ceased to be a presence there at that time. The stresses of his final years in the Shelbourne might have imposed some strains on his personal life. The following year, in 1974, Sally left him and he found himself bringing up his daughters alone. Although he retained his non-executive chairmanship of the Irish board of Trust House Forte his life became increasingly bound up in his work for the International Hotels Federation, which earned him well deserved international respect.

CHAPTER ELEVEN

THE PATRIOT GAME

'I learned all my life cruel England to blame
And now I am part of the Patriot Game'
Dominic Behan

By 1974, bomb scares had become a feature of Dublin life. Like many other institutions the Shelbourne had perfected an evacuation drill which was put into effect to empty the premises whenever a warning came but frequent repetition meant that many people did not take the alarms seriously any more. On the afternoon of 17 May 1974, members of the Shelbourne staff were coming off duty. Among them was Christina O'Loughlin, generally known as Chrissie, who worked in the hotel as a French polisher. Several of the departing staff turned to walk down Kildare Street and Chrissie walked with them for a while but she seemed in a hurry to get home that day. Nobody ever found out why. She outstripped her dawdling colleagues and walked on briskly to Nassau Street, where she crossed over the wall of Trinity College. As there was a bus strike that day, more cars than usual were parked along the college railings. The other Shelbourne employees who were following had just reached the corner of Kildare Street and Nassau Street when the car bomb exploded. Fifty-one year old Chrissie was one of the thirty-three people who died as a result of the bombings in Dublin and Monaghan that day. Hundreds were injured, many seriously. The tragedy invested future bomb scares in the hotel with a starker reality.

For Padraic Browne and his family a surreal episode came out of the blue a few months later. It was an August morning at the end of Horse Show week and the hotel had, as usual, been hectic. Padraic's wife, Terry, had been busy too, trying to finish off her last batches of jams and chutneys for the store cupboard before the family left for their summer holiday in Waterville the next day. The Browne's eighteen year old daughter, Joanne, was waiting for the results of her Leaving Certificate. In a tense scenario, undoubtedly reproduced in thousands of homes that morning she was sitting on the staircase watching the letter box. Her mother, ostensibly busy in the kitchen with her preserving pots, was keeping her ears open for the post too.

When a brown envelope dropped onto the mat Joanne leapt on it like a cat on a bird. Terry, listening with bated breath in the kitchen heard the ominous sound of weeping and hurried out to give consolation. The letter in her daughter's hand was so alarming that the Leaving Certificate results, the preparations for the Waterville holiday and the bubbling chutney pot were completely forgotten. They read it together:

> I. Mr. Browne, on reading the first lines of this communication your natural reaction may be to telephone the police. DO NOT. Complete reading our document. Consider the consequences for your establishment and your wife and children in the event of non compliance with our requirements.
>
> II. We have placed three (3) explosive devices at positions in your establishment designed to maximise structural damage and ensure that it will be extremely difficult to locate them in the available time. These are radio activated devices which cannot detonate prematurely or

spontaneously. If our requirements are not fully complied with we will detonate the devices by remote control. This will cause serious structural damage, general fire damage, possible loss of life and extremely damaging publicity.

III. Our basic requirements are as follows; (Your detailed instructions will come later) £60,000 in used Irish currency notes to be delivered in bundles of £1,000 and made up approximately as follows

100 x 1 = 100

30 x 10 =300

20 x 20 =400

40 x 5 = 200

IV. At this point we give you some information about ourselves which may help you to come to a quick decision favourable to both of us. We are not concerned with ideologies. We are an international group. We owe no commitment to Dublin, Ireland North or South or any political party or grouping within it and will have no hesitation whatsoever in taking this action to its ultimate conclusion.

V. We see your options as follows and our reactions.

(a) You contact the police immediately and initiate a full scale alert involving a search of the premises. It will be immediately obvious to us that you are not complying with our demands and in that case the devices will be triggered immediately.

(b) You may consider our demands and endeavour with or without police co-operation to search for the devices. There will be constant surveillance of the Hotel and any attempt to handle the problem in this manner will come immediately to our notice and the consequences will be as already outlined.

(c) You co-operate fully. In that event the operation will never be repeated and will receive on our part absolutely no publicity.

VI. To summarise: I think we have made our position clear. All of your possible reactions have been taken into account and in the event of a serious deviation from our instructions the consequences have been [made] clear. In addition to your hotel the safety of your wife and children should enter into your considerations. In par.

VII We give more detailed instructions and comment further on the consequences of non-compliance.

VII. You will be contacted at the hotel at 12 o'clock today with the code word Consolidated Edison. In subsequent dealings this will be abbreviated to Con Edison.

(b) You must not deviate from the route which will be given to you

(c) You must not leave the public thoroughfare save in accordance with our instructions.

(d) You must not speak to anyone no matter how briefly or casually.

(e) You must not use a kiosk telephone

(f) After delivering the money you must return to the hotel by the same route complying with all of the above requirements.

(g) The currency notes must not be marked in any way, i.e. (I) on the face to enable identification. (II) In any other manner designed to facilitate detection such as photographic optical or other similar methods involving light outside the visible spectrum. (III) The serial numbers of the notes must not be recorded.

A special word of warning is called for here as this is the aspect of the operation over which we have control. We will have facilities for carrying out an immediate random check on the notes. If it should prove positive it will be regarded as total non-compliance with the attendant circumstances. If, after the conclusion of our action we discover you to be in breach of our conditions with regards to the currency the operation will be repeated and the second without demands being made or warnings given.

VIII To conclude: Bear in mind that from now on you are being kept under surveillance. Any one of your staff, guests or passers by in the street may be our agents, none of these will carry anything on his/her person to indicate such. Apprehension or arrest is therefore either impossible or acting directly against your own interest as failure of our agents to report will be regarded as due to your agency.

A final caution do not attempt to upset our timetable by claiming inability to have the cash available on time.

It is hard to understand how anyone, in 1974, could expect a hotel manager to find £60,000 in cash, but terrorists' demands do not welcome discussion.

Padraic Browne (on right) escorting Pierre Trudeau through the lobby.

Within a few hours, Padraic Browne, presented with this dilemma, contacted the Gardaí. By lunchtime he felt as though he was taking part in a spy movie. His family had been removed from their home. The location which was chosen for their protective custody was the Shelbourne which was, allegedly, stuffed with explosives, but could not be evacuated for fear of upsetting the extortionists. Browne himself was making his way by a prescribed route to the South County Hotel, wired with a concealed walkie-talkie radio and lugging a weighty briefcase. The ransom money had been mocked up by cutting wads of paper to the requisite size and taping genuine bank notes to the front and back of each bundle.

Sixty thousand pounds was enough to buy half a dozen suburban family houses so, even allowing for the fake notes, enclosed in each bundle there was still a fair sum in the case. Having sat around for a while in the South County a telephone message from Con Edison sent him trailing off on another circuitous route. At eight that evening he found himself, still wired and clutching the briefcase, in the lounge of the Gresham Hotel.

The cloak and dagger day seemed to have gone on forever. He had expected to be at home by this time, preparing for an early departure to Waterville on the morrow. He glanced around the quiet room, convinced that here, at last, the contact would be made. He scrutinised the handful of people relaxing in the adjacent armchairs and concluded, eventually, that the only person who was not patently above suspicion was a tallish nun whose features were obscured by a capacious wimple. The all concealing habit, he realised immediately, was one of the classic disguises for resistance fighters, invading paratroopers, terrorists and the like. He edged towards the veiled figure and initiated a conversation, encrypting some pointed remarks to alert the criminal to the fact that his camouflage had been penetrated. The nun, perturbed by his approaches rose and made a hasty exit. As she did so the farewells of the staff made it clear that Sister Rita was well known to them.

Shortly afterwards Padraic Browne was called to take another telephone call. He was still fuming over his *faux pas* with Sister Rita from Tipperary and he listened incredulously as Con Edison instructed him that his next rendezvous point should be an isolated spot on the Curragh, after dark. It occurred to Browne that although he had just disobeyed the terrorists' directives by communicating with the nun they were unaware of the fact so he was obviously not under close surveillance. If that was the case perhaps the rest of the extortion demand was a tissue of creative fantasies too. It was an inspiring moment. He told Con Edison to 'get stuffed' and carted his briefcase of money back to the Shelbourne. Nothing more was ever heard of Con Edison and the life of the Browne family and the hotel returned to normal.

When a bomb actually did explode in the Shelbourne, two years later, Browne was in hospital. He had been advised to relax after a recent illness.

A television set had been installed in the room to provide undemanding entertainment, a rare enough commodity in hospitals in 1976. On the evening of Friday, 13 May, he turned it on just in time to hear that a massive bomb had just exploded in the Shelbourne. It set his convalescence back by weeks.

The death of Frank Stagg, a Provisional IRA hunger striker who had died in Wakefield prison was followed by a number of reprisals. Several incendiary bombs damaged property in Dublin on that Friday. The Shelbourne, owned by a British Company, Trust House Forte was perceived as a legitimate target for a political gesture.

The bomb was planted in the Leech Suite on the mezzanine behind the lift shaft. At that time the former site of Mr McCurdy's winter garden was always referred to as the vestibule. When the warning, allowing only forty minutes, was telephoned to the hotel switchboard, the device was spotted almost immediately. It was in a briefcase under a side table. One of the porters, Michael O'Dowd, tried to grab it and remove it from the building. Fortunately his reflex of gallantry was restrained by colleagues and the evacuation began immediately The operation was so fast and efficient that all the guests and most of the staff were out half an hour before the explosion.

The only casualty was the duty manager, Dennis Friel. Like the captain of a sinking ship he had been checking and double checking in every area to make sure that no stragglers had been overlooked. As he galloped through the front door, at the last possible moment, the blast struck. He was lifted off his feet and propelled half way across the street, where for a few tense seconds he lay stunned and bleeding. Colleagues rushed to help him to his feet. He was unaware that his back was peppered with shards of glass until he groped around with his hand to investigate an odd sensation of warmth and wetness. His reaction was stoic. As he felt the damage to his

Dennis Friel, the only person injured in the explosion.

shredded garments then stared at the blood running off his fingers he said disgustedly, 'Ah, Jaysus, wouldn't you know I'd be in my best suit.'

The damage was significant. The corner of the building adjacent to the north west of the Leech Suite was demolished and the plate glass windows overlooking both St Stephen's Green and Kildare Street were blown out. The interior was devastated. Every member of the staff rallied round. Shifts were forgotten as they swept broken glass by day and night and restored a semblance of order. The phoenix arose from the ashes in two days and the Shelbourne opened again for business on the Sunday.

Apart from the renovation work, one significant architectural alteration took place as a result of the bomb. The staircase leading from the side door in Kildare Street to the mezzanine area was removed as a security risk. Safety precautions in the hotel were redoubled. Hand baggage was inspected at the door and the days of leaving parcels and luggage at the porter's desk were over.

The assassination of the British Ambassador Christopher Ewart Biggs and Judith Cooke, a senior civil servant from the Northern Ireland office, in July of 1976, was a further blow to the British tourist market and did nothing to promote peace of mind in British-owned institutions like the Shelbourne. The place was, in the words of the Chinese curse, 'living in interesting times'. Danger can be a stimulant, however, sharpening minds and heightening enjoyment. As Orson Welles, literally one of the biggest stars ever to reside in the Shelbourne, pointed out, Italy, under the violent sway of the Borgias was the cradle of the Renaissance. The Swiss, on the other hand 'had brotherly love, five hundred years of peace and democracy and what did that produce? The cuckoo clock.'

People were still having fun at the Shelbourne, and it attracted a high proportion of those intrepid tourists who were still willing to brave the hazards of Dublin. Throughout the summer season it offered first class entertainment. From 1974 to 1979 the summer supper theatre, which was presented in the ballroom, was booked out for six nights a week. Noel Pearson produced the sophisticated, cabaret style musicals which included *Jacques Brel Is Alive And Well And Living in Paris*, *Side By Side By Sondheim* and *The Fantasticks.* Rosaleen Linehan, John Kavanagh, Niall Tobín and Gay Byrne were amongst the stars who featured.

Noel Keelehan's trio were the featured entertainment in the main dining room where there was a small dance floor and, once Earl Gill's television career led him into other paths Ray Allen took over the music in the ballroom. The Saddle Room was still one of the city's finest restaurants and the facilities of the Horseshoe Bar had been augmented by the opening of the Paddock Bar in the former Girl's Friendly Society building in number 34 Stephen's Green. The Paddock Bar boasted a rare amenity for the city centre which made it particularly popular during the summer. The rear doors opened on to a walled garden, a private oasis of tranquillity just yards away from the traffic in St Stephen's Green.

By 1979, three years after the mezzanine bomb, life in the city seemed to have resumed its old tenor, then, during August, Lord Louis Mountbatten was assassinated in Donegal Bay. The breakfast shift in the Shelbourne felt a sense of personal loss. The family had been in the hotel only a few weeks previously, hale and hearty and looking forward to their holiday. Now three of their party were dead and others injured. The Mountbatten family's routine on their visits to Sligo had never varied. The first stop on their Irish summer holiday was always a leisurely breakfast in the Shelbourne. Since the drive-on car ferry had started service in 1965 cross channel travellers were on the road much earlier than in the days when cars were hoisted up and swung on to the wharf by crane.

The Mountbatten party usually occupied four or five cars and these would be left parked on the opposite side of the road while they ate. Security was negligible, with never more than two security men and frequently only one. The family were always in good spirits when setting out for their summer home in Mullaghmore. Lord Mountbatten would stride into the lobby, announcing: 'Here we are again' and after breakfast there were handshakes all round as they left for Sligo.

In September of that year, Pope John Paul II made a visit to Ireland and about a third of the country's population assembled in the Phoenix Park for his Mass there. The occasion was freely available to everyone except infants, a prohibition which did not help to reconcile the parents of Ireland's youngest citizens to the Vatican's hard line on contraception. At some point in his visit, the Pope was served a crème brulée, the signature pudding of the Shelbourne, which had been introduced to the menu by pastry chef, Alan Gleeson. The Pope is said to have enjoyed it so much that he subsequently had it flown to Rome for his consumption. Alan Gleeson has no specific recollection of making a pudding for shipment to Rome but says that it is possible he did, since requests for the pudding, the recipe and demonstrations of the method poured in by the dozen every week.

A stack of photocopied recipes was kept permanently on hand in the kitchen to meet the demands of people sampling the dish for the first time. The dish was adopted by Aer Lingus for first class travellers and, much more recently, Pierce Brosnan was one of those who asked for a live demonstration to accompany the recipe sheet. Crème brulée was a simple and classic dish in which a real vanilla custard, combined with whipped cream, was caramelised on top with a hot poker or salamander and served warm. At the time when it was first introduced, chefs in the hotel were still working on solid fuel ranges. Coal boys carried scuttles up and down from the basement all day long and there were no labour-saving devices to assist in the cooking process. The menus of the day indicate that the dessert trolley featured mainly traditional favourites; pies, gateaux, meringues, fruit and ice cream. Crèpes Suzette was the only individually made hot pudding available and that was not only exotic but expensive. The addition of crème brulée to the dining room menu was a touch of genius.

Alan Gleeson started his career in the hotel kitchens in 1948 and became the pastry chef in 1953, a position which he occupied for thirty years. His family typify the sort of dynastic loyalty which the Shelbourne was capable of attracting. His father, Leo, was with the hotel for over forty years from 1919. He was described by *Harper's* magazine as the best head porter in the world and he became the first head porter in Ireland to attain membership of the *International Societé des Cléfs d'Or*, an honour which would later be extended to Jimmy Dixon and others. Alan Gleeson's brother also did his culinary training in the Shelbourne and his nephew, Kenneth, became the third generation of the family to start his career there in 1970.

Horse Show week was still hectic but its pre-eminence in the year's social calendar was slipping into decline. British visitors, who had injected some variety into the circle of familiar resident faces, no longer came in such large numbers. Political unrest, the wealth tax, the fuel crisis and changing attitudes all combined to dent the old charmed circle. Young women who had been battery bred for early matrimony were becoming liberated. Being packaged in pastel tulle and marketed off to the highest bidder was no longer their only option. Dances were fewer and far less exclusive and boisterous behaviour often degenerated into brawls. Pouring the champagne from the balcony had been bad enough but once the bottles started to be thrown down too, things had gone too far.

By the end of the decade, the Horse Show hunt ball was looking like an anachronism. Broadcaster and writer David Hanly immortalised a typical Galway Blazers bash in his picaresque novel, *In Guilt And In Glory*, published in 1979. The Blazers, quite rightly, had the reputation of being the wildest night of the week. The account in the novel was drawn directly from his own experience. Shortly before writing the book he had procured tickets for visiting American friends to attend the Blazers' ball. They were interested in sampling the tribal rites of Anglo-Ireland at first hand. He escorted them to the Horseshoe Bar where the pre-ball booze-up was in full swing. They were so intimidated by the vigour of this preamble that they refused to go through with it alone and insisted he accompany them to the dance. As he tells it:

> The din in the Horseshoe Bar was almost soporific but the quality of the sound was quite different from the familiar clamour of Irish pubs late at night. The pitch was more strident, the greetings raucous and unselfconscious. The smoke was from thick cigars and it mingled with the smell of expensive perfumes above the small packed throng.

The trepidation of the Americans was understandable. They were witnessing an anthropological curiosity worthy of *National Geographic.* Hanly was quite willing to see the evening through with them but he was dressed in a pepper and salt tweed suit and evening dress was a rigid requirement for admittance to the ballroom. The Americans were equally adamant. He must come. It was a dilemma. He stared around the escalating racket of the Horseshoe Bar seeking inspiration:

> The clamour had increased, the cigar smoke had thickened, in spite of the air conditioning of which the hotel was inordinately proud. The high honking voices demanded attention from the barman and from companions and the buzz was frequently eclipsed by blasts of eldritch laughter. Gins and tonics plopped over rims and onto arms, to the floor, thick bullets of cigar ash fell on shoulders, faces grew red from drink and laughter, eyes teared, the whole bar was in a continuous explosion of industrious gaiety. The unmistakeable noises of Horse Show week.

Suddenly a dinner-jacketed figure materialised, neat, tidy and sober amongst the baying throng. It was an assistant manager. In the din, Hanly managed to convey the nature of his problem. The solution was swift and simple. The manager removed his jacket, shirt and tie on the spot and swapped them for Hanly's. In such a crush, he pointed out, any discrepancies below the waist would probably pass unnoticed. They did. Hanly went to the ball in brown brogues and hairy tweed trousers topped by a formal dinner jacket and the manager carried on his evening's duties in the reverse mismatch of clothing.

From there on Hanly's fictional dance adhered pretty closely to the real thing. A nervous horse is ridden round the dance floor and food and ice cubes are pelted about the room. The stock 'characters' of Horse Show week are all present, presiding squiffily over their tables. Nobody is sober and alcohol abuse reaches new levels of ingenuity as the night progresses. Geysers of champagne and Coca Cola are squirted over expensive clothes and coiffures. Some people pass out into merciful oblivion, others get sick. The most incredible aspect of the evening is that everyone has paid to be there.

After one such Blazers' dance in the seventies, the party who had sat at Lady Cusack-Smith's table reconvened later in more sober circumstances in the court. An argument in the ballroom, late in the evening, had spilled out on to the front steps at which point the fantasy world of the Horse Show collided with harsher realities. Three indignant dinner-jacketed antagonists found themselves being handcuffed and bundled into a paddy wagon which took them to cool off in the Harcourt Terrace garda station. Unfortunately, they were all plausible enough to get a quick release after which they regrouped with some of their earlier companions and continued the altercation.

It was a night of mayhem. When the case was heard in the Circuit Criminal Court in February 1977 one newspaper headline screamed 'After the Ball – Blood.' Several members of the hunt ball party were called to give evidence. Adrian Hardiman SC was the junior counsel for the defence. He still recalls it as one of the most confusing and colourful cases of his career. During a break in the first day's proceedings he telephoned some of his friends from UCD and advised them to get down to the Four Courts as quickly as possible since the proceedings in hand were more entertaining than a farce. Although all the witnesses had spent the evening together no two accounts of the evening's events tallied in any single particular.

The presiding Judge, Mr O'Flaherty, seemed, initially, as bemused as the counsel by the conflicting evidence which was so confidently and coherently dredged from the alcoholic lees of a Blazers' Hunt Ball. For the jury it was surreal. Jury service had recently been democratised to embrace non-property owners and they found it difficult to understand why key witnesses enjoyed apparently lavish lifestyles with no visible means of support. It had not taken O'Flaherty long to recognise the lineaments of decadence. When the time came for his peroration he told the jury that the prosecution witnesses were, for the most part, idle people, prepared to eke out a living on the remnants of their landed estates. At that point, the instructing solicitor for the defence left, explaining to Adrian Hardiman that he was an old man and could no longer stand that sort of excitement. The jury, after lengthy deliberations, felt unable to convict anyone. It was the end of an era.

CHAPTER TWELVE

FIN DE SIÈCLE

Tempting one always to prolong one's visit.

Nineteen eighty-three was a watershed for the Shelbourne. To begin with, the normal round of cultural, social and sporting occasions kept the place humming. Early in the year, Hamish Hamilton hosted a joint book launch for three of their Irish authors: Peter Somerville-Large, Clare Boylan and Gerald Hanley. Clare Boylan was publishing her first novel *Holy Pictures* and Gerald Hanley's *Noble Descents* was to be his last. Among the many writers who frequented the hotel Gerald Hanley was among the most significant. His experiences in Africa, India and Japan furnished the settings for his chronicles of imperial decay and Hemingway and Burgess were among his many fellow authors who held his work in high esteem. However he never translated his preoccupation with the end of the Empire into the context of his native country. Perhaps that is why he is less readily classified as an 'Irish' writer than some of his contemporaries. He was, in fact, a genuinely international novelist whose view of the political convulsions of the century was informed by his own nationality and his ability to listen to others with tolerance and discretion.

Later that year, during the summer the Cotton Jury clan re-grouped for the wedding of Sally and Peter Jury's daughter, Sophie, to the film production manager Steve Tebbit. Both Peter and Sally were now resident abroad. It was the last Cotton Jury family party to be held in the Shelbourne.

The advent of autumn initiated some major changes in the character of the hotel. Inevitably, in its long history, the Shelbourne had encountered its share of vicissitudes. Christian Goodman's terminal decline in health, so soon after the completion of the new building, had been followed by other abrupt departures. Charles Stuart Parnell's father died suddenly in the hotel, having contracted a chill at a cricket match. Despite the unexpected nature of his sudden decline he had the presence of mind to summon a solicitor in order to disinherit his daughter, Anna, whose political activities had displeased him. Suicide was not unknown amongst the guests. Several staff members, like the egregious Mr Olden died in harness. Barney Molloy, too, was found dead in his apartment over the Shelbourne garage by his racing crony, hotel resident Frank Sheedy at the end of a normal working day. In 1948, Seamus Pilow, a fourteen-year-old page boy, died in a shooting accident in the basement. Head lounge waiter, Bill Daly, had entered the room just in time to identify the object with which two of the boys were playing when it went off. In 1983, although there were no fatalities, the hotel sustained the greatest loss of staff in its history.

Up to that point there had been just three strikes: the first in 1920 followed by the General Strike of 1922, which had been an ineluctable experience for all Dublin employers and a third, short dispute in 1959. This was occasioned when a Frenchman, Louis Verat, was engaged on a two-year contract to train in a new restaurant manager. At the end of the term both Verat and Peter Jury were inclined to prolong the arrangement but Jack McMenamin, the trainee, was ready for his long awaited promotion. The staff supported McMenamin's position and posited that Irish staff should not be passed over in favour of foreigners.

The strike lasted for about ten days while directors and management mucked in to keep the show on the road. Every day the Drogheda-based director, Colonel Cairns, brought in eggs and milk from his farm.

His response to the crisis was typical of what Dennis Wrangham had praised as 'the commonsense and warm humanity of Tom Cairns'. His positive contributions to the board over the years had always reflected much of the practical, pioneering spirit of his famous forebear, yachtsman Willie Jameson of the distilling family. Padraic Browne and Eoin Dillon drove the hotel van out to Blackrock at dawn each day to collect bakery bread for breakfast. Sally Jury moved into the laundry and washed non-stop for the duration. Smooth running in the laundry affected more than just the Shelbourne since all the linen from the Hibernian was sent there too. The hotel never closed as the official staff were able to provide a skeleton service for guests. Service was confined to bed and breakfast for the duration of the strike and everyone took turns helping with the dining room and other basic services. One of the receptionists, now running a guest-house in Austria, remembers it as an enjoyable experience:

'Please do not pass our picket.'

> The hotel management at the time were very kind and, as far as I can remember, we got a week's extra pay and a week's extra holidays.

Meanwhile Dennis McGeary negotiated a satisfactory solution. Jack McMenamin was installed as restaurant manager, and remained in the post for many years.

This co-operative spirit did not characterise the dispute of 1983. That was a grimmer business, symptomatic of the political and financial instability that afflicted the whole country throughout the eighties. Nineteen seventy-nine had set the first record for industrial disputes in the history of the State and from there on things went downhill, to the point where the Republic was rated, along with Italy's Mezzogiorno, as the most disadvantaged area in the EEC. The economy was in dire straits. Jobs were vanishing like morning dew and inflation had reached twenty per cent by late 1981. The government response to this fiscal mismanagement did not reconcile the work force to the considerable challenge of making ends meet. The electorate were enjoined to tighten their belts. Taxpayers, who had spent the seventies doing just that while interest rates soared, were told that they had been living beyond their means and that every man, woman and child in the population had now accrued an individual debt of several thousand pounds in foreign loans. The public was not happy.

The staff at the Shelbourne were no less affected than anyone else by the uncertain times. International hotel work seemed a less secure career option than formerly. In February 1982 Forte's other flagship hotel in Dublin, the Royal Hibernian, had been closed, after two hundred and thirty one years in business, releasing a highly trained staff on to a torpid job market. The Hibernian had fallen victim to the commercial pragmatism of the day. Its foundation predated that of the Shelbourne and the cost of renovating the venerable and gracious building to conform with health and safety regulations was deemed unfeasible when compared to the development value of the site.

In April of 1983 the annual wages increment, which had been eagerly awaited, was announced. Some of the staff were disappointed to find that they had been awarded a mere £1. The climate was ripe for trouble and it started with a dispute in the Paddock Bar. Then, as now, management trainees needed to become familiar with every aspect of the hotel's operations. One of them had been allocated to assist Joe Tyndall, the head barman in the Paddock Bar. They did not see eye to eye and Tyndall conveyed his reluctance to continue the arrangement to Marcello Giobbi, who was the manager at the time. Management insisted that the trainee should be re-instated. Neither side would budge. Tyndall was asked to leave the bar and declined to do so. The management then sent in the Gardaí to physically remove Tyndall from the bar where he was still working. The staff were outraged by what they perceived as an over-reaction to the argument and walked out on a three day unofficial strike. When they returned they were unable to gain access as there was a management lock out.

The hotel was closed from September until early December. By late October the terms and conditions under which employees could recommence work during December had been negotiated. The ITGWU recommended that their members should accept these as it had been made quite clear that further negotiations would be not resumed and the same proposals would be put on the table again the following March. Marcello Giobbi circulated a letter to each employee making it clear that the management felt as aggrieved as the staff:

> The Shelbourne Hotel has suffered a set back which has damaged its reputation as a great hotel. To recover will require hard work, determination and sacrifice on the part of management and staff. Our task will be to convince our customers:
>
> that they will never again be inconvenienced by a close down.
>
> that the quality of service and attention will be better than ever before.
>
> that the hotel will maintain standards equal to … or better than … those of any five star hotel in the world.
>
> These are not easy objectives, but we must achieve them if the success of the Shelbourne is to be assured in the future.
>
> The survival package, designed to secure the FUTURE LIFE of a prosperous Shelbourne with the protection of jobs provides for…

> A GUARANTEE that staff returning to work will not earn less than they did before the strike.
> NEW pay structures
> New work practices based on customers' needs and designed to IMPROVE JOB SATISFACTION.
> IMPROVED sick pay scheme.
> A Fair Distribution of service charge based on a SINGLE POOL system.
> In the event of jobs not being available for all who wish to return to work, a voluntary redundancy will apply.

The trade union document was more detailed, including the new rates of pay, which ranged from £30 per week for a first year commis and £34 for page boys to £80 or £90 for administrative posts or heads of department. Pay levels and structures were effectively unchanged but many long serving staff, whose re-employment would probably have been secure, opted to take redundancy before the cut off date of 7 November. They felt that the working conditions outlined would be less flexible and more exacting, with split shifts of up to thirteen hours and a threat to their established routines in conditions such as:

> Rosters will be agreed by the Head of Department and the Personnel Manager and issued two weeks in advance.
> All existing work practices are cancelled; new job descriptions will be issued and; All staff will be rostered over a 90 hour fortnight to include meal breaks of 1 hour per shift or 1/2 hour per split shift.

Staff members returning to work were necessarily reduced in numbers as certain amenities had disappeared forever. The Paddock Bar, the Saddle Room and the Grill never re-opened after the strike. The voluntary redundancy package allowed for a maximum of 123 employees to terminate their employment. It was a very large proportion of the total staff.

There were other, more subtle changes in the character of the slimmed down Shelbourne. Since the nineteenth century, when the Irish Rugby Football Club had featured in Margaret Cotton Jury's list of debtors, rugby players and supporters had treated the hotel as an unofficial clubhouse. As an old Rugbeian himself Peter Jury had fostered the relationship and the Shelbourne had virtually monopolised the business generated by the Five Nations Tournament and post match celebrations. Beds in the Shelbourne for these occasions had been so highly prized that people had preferred to take a screened off bunk in 120 or one of the other first floor reception rooms, rather than book more spacious and private accommodation elsewhere.

The eighties saw teams and followers alike becoming diffused around the town but many of the former stars of the rugby pitch continued to come and go. Many of them, like Dr A.J.F. O'Reilly had become key players in other international games after retiring from the sport. Business had become glamorous. Its élite had supplanted the old *Burke's* and *Debrett's* set as the repositories of power and influence. They formed natural alliances with politicians, speaking the same language and often sharing a common background. The Horseshoe Bar was the cradle of this symbiosis. It offered privacy and discretion and Jimmy Kelly, the head barman whose career there spanned thirty years, ensured that the surroundings were always civilised. He barred mobile phones and raucous behaviour and was generally inflexible in matters of bar etiquette. Nobody, however important, was allowed to breach his rules. His policies paid off. In 1985 *Newsweek International* took a poll in which the Horseshoe Bar was voted one of best hundred bars worldwide.

Among the power-brokers frequenting it P.J. Mara, Government Press Officer and sometime senator, was one of the most influential. As spin doctor to Charles J. Haughey he kept a low profile until the satirical radio programme, *Scrap Saturday*, turned him into a household name. The Horseshoe Bar, only a few minutes walk from his office in Government Buildings, was the place where he socialised with his wide circle of acquaintances from professional, business, entertainment and media circles.

Journalist Declan Lynch described his peripatetic lifestyle:

> As someone who probably thinks that a desk is just something for putting your feet on P.J.'s office is perpetually on the move, a walking-talking ferment of bonhomie, gadding around Leinster House, the Shelbourne, the media haunts of Merrion Row or the exalted inner sanctum of U2 concerts.

Noel Pearson in the Horseshoe Bar (photo Sarah Owens).

With friends like Noel Pearson and Eamon Dunphy he invested the Horseshoe Bar with the atmosphere of a club. When he was put up for membership of the nearby Kildare Street and University Club in 1988 Michael O'Toole wrote in his *Evening Press* column:

> The important thing about P.J.'s prospective membership of the Kildare Street and University Club is the blow that will be struck to the Horseshoe Bar of the Shelbourne. Poor Lord Forte won't know what has hit him and Jimmy Kelly (the head barman) will probably go into mourning.

The fact that Jimmy Kelly retired the following year after thirty years of service was probably not directly related to Mr Mara's new membership of the Kildare Street and University Club. After the management of the Horseshoe Bar had passed into the hands of Seán Boyd, who still presides there, he remained a regular attendant.

With the strike of 1983 settled the Shelbourne started to re-consolidate, holding a gala ball to celebrate one hundred and sixty years in business and playing host in 1984 to the European Heads of State attending the EEC summit in Dublin Castle. The refurbishment of the lobby was completed in preparation for the latter occasion. The lobby fireplace, which had been ripped out in the first heady euphoria of central heating was reinstated. Winter arrivals came in from the wet streets to the welcoming blaze of a real fire, flanked by capacious sofas. A portrait by Eve Castelli was hung above the mantelpiece. The subject was Catherine O'Reilly, known to her circle as 'Aisling' the name which was attached for many years to the hotel's restaurant.

Gala 160-year Anniversary Ball.

On the face of it the Shelbourne had overcome its problems and was back in the saddle but, only three years after the 1983 strike had been settled, another dispute arose, this time over pay and conditions. It lasted a full six months. In October, the month when Garret FitzGerald admitted that the Exchequer owed over £20 billion, the largest per capita debt in the world in relation to the population, the Shelbourne workers came out on strike. It was an unusually harsh winter for the twenty-four hour pickets which were manned outside the hotel. On Christmas Day the Siberian front was temporarily alleviated by supporters who drove to the hotel with car loads of invigorating food and drink, but, for the most part, it was a lean vigil. Eventually the hierarchy intervened as mediators. Workers, returning to indoor duties after months of exposure to the elements, were alarmed to find themselves sloughing their weather-beaten outdoor skins like snakes in the centrally heated atmosphere. One former striker claims to have shed his epidermis at least six times before he re-acclimatised himself but still insists that the mental rehabilitation was far more slow and painful.

Marcello Giobbi had left the hotel in 1985 to be succeeded by Alan Blest. Nevertheless, the commitments guaranteed in his missive to the strikers of 1983 continued to be honoured:

> Thanks to the faith of THF in the Shelbourne Hotel and its staff, the enormous capital expenditure refurbishing banqueting areas and all bedrooms continues ...

Gerald Lawless had become manager when, in 1989 a colossal renovation of the ballroom took place and Michael Scott's galleried circus tent was transformed into John Hunt's Great Room. The scheme had been determined at the end of 1988. Originally it had been intended to increase the ballroom area by extending it over the walled garden but feasibility studies, at that time, decided that the garden was a an amenity of more environmental importance than a larger ballroom area. The former Paddock Bar was, at this stage, renamed the Garden Room and its refurbishment was the first phase of the re-development. Once completed the Garden Room became a self-contained suite which could operate independently of the hotel. The second stage of the development was the addition of more reception rooms to the newly conceived Great Room complex. These were the former Shelbourne Rooms, which kept their old name but were given a more flexible new bar area.

Finally the ballroom itself was remodelled in a way which would house conferences or presentations as easily as the traditional grand ball. The overall style is neo-Georgian, echoing the architectural motifs of the Garden Room and Shelbourne Rooms. Features such as the Doric columns and the fibrous plasterwork and joinery were all copied or adapted from earlier designs in the building.

In 1991 the former Saddle Room, which had been more or less relegated to the status of a storeroom, re-opened as the Shelbourne Bar. It was high time that the Horseshoe Bar's facilities were supplemented. The bar which had once provided a quiet meeting place for the movers and shakers of Irish society had become crowded. The activities of the regular clients had become gossip column fodder and that, in turn, had attracted gawpers whom Eamon Dunphy described as 'all kinds of chancers.'

On one evening he, Noel Pearson and P.J. Mara arrived in for a quiet drink and found no seats available. Mara complained to his companions: 'I feel like I'm in the Zoological Gardens when I come in here now. All these yuppies are coming in for is just to look at us.' The Shelbourne Bar provided a spacious retreat for the overflow. The false ceiling, which had been installed in the days of the Saddle Room, was removed and the original plasterwork exposed, returning the room to McCurdy's original proportions.

Trust House Forte became Forte plc in 1991. Its policies of expansion and acquisitions continued. In 1992 the company entered into a joint venture with AGIP for the management of eighteen hotels in Italy and in 1994 it bought the Meridien group. This international hotel chain originally evolved when Air France merged their own subsidiary, Relais Aeriens Français with Hotels France International. After the first oil crisis Le Meridien had started developing facilities for business and corporate clientele in the Middle East. The second oil crisis saw it expanding into North America and, subsequently, the Asian Pacific Rim. When Air France's financial situation deteriorated during the early 1990s the EU Commission in Brussels made a directive in 1994, that the airline should sell any subsidiaries which were not directly connected with air traffic. In November 1994, when the takeover was done, nobody would have guessed that Forte itself would soon fall prey to a hostile takeover bid from Granada. Ironically it might have been the acquisition of Meridien, creating a global upscale in Forte's hotel network and providing a strong foundation for future growth which made the company an attractive acquisition for Granada.

Just two months before the Shelbourne, as part of the Forte group, found itself embroiled in the takeover battle, the Side Door Restaurant was opened. Since the Grill room closed in the 1983 strike this area had been used as a staff facility. It was now renovated to provide a reasonably priced alternative to the main dining room. Barry McCabe's design for the interior was less formal than the other public areas with oak floors, cream walls and art deco wooden tables and chairs. The floor at the rear of the room was raised by a few feet to create a split level. The large, lantern effect lights lining the walls were commissioned from students at the National College of Art and Design. The opening of the Side Door in October 1995 completed the rehabilitation of the ground floor rooms for public use.

In December, Granada opened their offensive on Forte with a bid of approximately £3.1 billion. The precise sum varied according to fluctuations in Granada's share price. The board of Forte considered this offer to be undervalued. Forte shareholders were circulated with documents by both sides. The date of 15 December 1995 was set as the closing date for Granada's first offer and 9 January was the final day for an increased bid. The closing date for shareholders to make their decision was 23 January, after which, if more than fifty per cent of shareholders had not accepted Granada's offer, the bid would lapse.

The time scale was tight. When Granada published its annual report it announced the date of its AGM as 24 January, one day after the closing date for acceptance of the offer. The decision on the offer was likely to be made very quickly on 23 January as nearly eighty per cent of Forte shares were in the hands of about thirty City fund management institutions.

By the end of 1995 aggressive propaganda campaigns were under way. The business pages of the press found that the battle provided excellent copy to fill the slack season of Christmas and New Year and opinions were divided as to who would ultimately be the victor in this King Kong/ Godzilla style confrontation.

Regular bulletins, entitled Defence News were circulated through the Forte Empire. The *Financial Times* of 9 December was unimpressed by an early edition of this publication:

> Forte's flimsy defence document adds little. Nonetheless the ability of Granada to launch an irresistible bid looks increasingly questionable.

In response to the threat from Granada, Forte proposed a strategy of disposal of non-core business and a de-merger of hotels and restaurants. The key initiatives were: the creation of a focused hotel company; the sale of restaurants and other businesses to a value of £2.2 billion; the de-merger of the Savoy; the revaluation of the hotels; and the repurchase of shares up to a value of £800 million. Proceeds from the sales programme would be used to return cash to shareholders. Although some commentators saw these proposals as insufficiently detailed and ultimately unexciting the move certainly gave shareholders food for thought. *The Independent* reported:

> For shareholders the decision is becoming a more finely balanced one than it looked at the outset ... Since then Forte has astonished all with its willingness to take on board quite radical break-up and re-structuring proposals. It has also achieved some success in undermining Granada's case which, given the quality and expense of bidder's advice has been put forward in an alarmingly sloppy and ill-thought-out way.

Employment strategies as well as finances were brought into play. When Forte vaunted its management flexibility by pointing out that seventy out of every hundred managers had joined the company in the previous five years Granada countered with the information that ninety-three percent of their own managerial staff rose from within the ranks of the system.

The whole bidding imbroglio was more in character with eighties-style *Liars' Poker* than the industrial logic of the nineties but Granada carried the day. On 25 January former Forte employees received a letter welcoming them to the Granada group and promising a straightforward management style, promotions on merit and a two way loyalty within the company. The Shelbourne was one of the many properties which passed into the control of Granada's Chief Executive, Donegal born Gerry Robinson. He was nine years old, the ninth in a family of ten children, when he left Dunfanaghy for England in 1959. His subsequent career took him on a straight trajectory from accounts clerk to one of Britain's most powerful businessmen. He was still in his thirties when he led a £168 million management buy-out of Grand Met's catering company, Compass, and assured his own personal wealth. In 1991 he became involved with Granada, the massive and diverse conglomerate with interests in everything from television to roadside catering. The group employs ninety-thousand people but its management style is far from cumbersome. The staff of the head office at Granada consists of only twenty four people. Gerry Robinson is one of Ireland's most successful and least publicised exports. He has never experienced any difficulties as an Irishman working in the city of London. On the contrary:

> There is something about coming in from the outside that is a help. Maybe it's because you don't fit into any stereotype. There have been no problems and no prejudice.

In many ways he is reminiscent of that earlier entrepreneurial Irishman connected to the Shelbourne, Martin Burke. He sees today's Ireland as a viable business environment:

> There is an acceptance of business here and it's easier to get good people. Attitudes have changed enormously here. It does feel very positive.

The strategy that led to Granada's acquisition of Forte was devised by Charles Allen. Like Gerry Robinson he has an impressive track record in business and enjoyed early success. He was only thirty-one when he was appointed managing director of Compass following the management buy-out and he managed their successful stock market flotation the following year. In 1996, the year when the Shelbourne passed into the ownership of Granada he became Granada Group Chief Executive.

While Le Meridien underwent two changes of ownership during 1995 and 1996 Jean Ricoux was managing one of their showcase operations in

Abu Dhabi, United Arab Emirates. This is a multi-product property including a hotel, a complex of studio residences, a health spa, eight restaurants and bars and a private resort club and beach. For over twenty years his career as an international hotelier had kept him expatriated and he and his family were ready to return to Europe. His two sons who were born when their father was working in Syria and Hong Kong, had never been based in their native continent. Alterations in the company heralded changes for the Ricoux family when Jean became the General Manager of the Shelbourne in August 1997 taking over from Donal O'Gallagher.

Jean Ricoux, the Shelbourne General Manager.

As a hotel dynasty the Ricoux family had much in common with the Cotton Jurys. In 1865, two years before the present Shelbourne Hotel was built, Jean's great-grandparents became proprietors of the Hôtel Les Messageries in Arbois, Burgundy, the home town of Louis Pasteur. It has remained in the family ever since and is now run by his brother, Serge. Jean's career has taken him further afield.

There had always been a family tradition of travelling while learning the business and Jean's training began in Switzerland, Germany and England. After that he spent ten years specialising in Sales and Marketing with Hilton International. He became Area Director for Sales for France, the Iberian Peninsula, North Africa and Malta before taking over the management of the Palmyra Meridien in Syria. In the course of his subsequent appointments in Hong Kong, Malaysia, Singapore and Sydney he moved through various hotel groups before rejoining Meridien in 1992 in Abu Dhabi. In that year he was also awarded the French National Order of Merit.

Immediately after arriving in Dublin he decided that the 175th Anniversary of the Shelbourne should be fittingly commemorated. In 1998 he presided over the opening of the Shelbourne Health and Leisure

Club in number 34 St Stephen's Green. The rooms overlooking the Green which had in turn been the Paddock Bar and the Garden Suite became the reception area and the swimming pool was constructed behind on the site of the garden. At last, health-conscious visitors like Charles Blair could keep in shape without risking life and limb in Dublin's traffic.

By early 1998, other plans were being implemented too. The refurbishment of the entire ground floor had been undertaken, in a scheme which embraced the Number 27 restaurant, the Lord Mayor's Lounge, the Horseshoe Bar, the Lobby and the Mezzanine. The second and third floor guestrooms have been given new interior schemes and a total renovation of the façade, overlooking St Stephen's Green and Kildare Street has been completed.

The preservation of the Shelbourne has taken place in an environment of unprecedented growth. The city around it is being reconstructed but has not yet lost its human scale. No canyons of skyscrapers have risen yet to dwarf the building which rose 'as tall as a cliff' in 1867 . It remains the *genus loci* at the heart of Joyce's 'gallant, venal city' and its upper levels still command a clear view of Dublin's encircling sea and mountains, although the intervening roofscape is bristling with construction cranes.

From the very beginning the place created an impression of permanence. Martin Burke's Shelbourne was less than twenty years old when Thackeray described it as a 'respectable old edifice' and she became 'The grand old lady of Stephen's Green' a century before political correctitude made verbal embellishments of brute gender offensive. It is an appropriate term for the maternal nurturing spirit which pervades the hotel. Like any matriarch of an extended family, the Shelbourne is too engaged with life to be haunted but the past still lingers.

Early morning in the Shelbourne is as lambent as a newly-minted coin. Polished calm has always superseded any gaieties of the preceding night. Breakfast in Number 27 is lavish and leisurely. Upstairs the house is as active as a beehive, with linen being refreshed, furniture waxed and rooms aired. By the time the breakfast chefs finish at ten-thirty the lunch staff have already become active in the kitchens and at eleven the Shelbourne Bar opens and experiences the quietest moment of its day before the lunchtime rush. Sitting in the Shelbourne Bar before noon gives the sort of prohibited pleasure that used to be attached to reading novels during the morning.

From twelve-thirty to three kitchens on the ground floor and the first floor seethe with activity as lunch is served in Number 27, the Side Door, the Shelbourne Bar, the Lord Mayor's Lounge and the first floor private suites. The tide of hungry humanity does not ebb until early afternoon and then, for a few hours, there is a lull. Tea time in the Lord Mayor's Lounge is muted and airbrushed by nostalgia. The chink of teacups and the cadences of Marie Whelan's piano are punctuated by the rhythmic sound of hoof beats as horse-drawn carriages bowl past the windows on sightseeing promenades.

The evening brings a return of activity with parties in the Great Room and a genial buzz filling every public room. Much later, in the stilly night, dreams take over. The Shelbourne never sleeps but, when the doors to the outside world have been closed, only a handful of night staff are left to man the labyrinth. They seem to tread more softly, as if ministering to invisible presences. They never number more than ten, more often there are no more than half a dozen of them. They are the night watch, manning approaches and patrolling the fire points along the sleeping corridors and past the deserted powerhouses of the administrative offices and kitchens. They share the night with the *lares* and *penates* of the Shelbourne's past.

Without the incessant grumble of passing traffic the clocks tick audibly. Even ashes falling from the grate assert themselves in the hush of night. It is the time when the echoes of old voices pervade the air of the upper corridors and silk seems to rustle down the empty staircase. The hours of regeneration and remembrance end with the dawn chorus of birds in St Stephen's Green. At half-five the outer doors are unbolted to admit trays of hot croissants, straight from the oven. The fragrance of freshly baked bread opens a new Shelbourne day.